MW01538910

MONTENEGRO TRAVEL

GUIDE 2025

Unveiling the Hidden Gem of the Balkans

Brad T. Watts

Copyright © Brad T. Watts

All rights reserved. No part of this publication may be reproduced, distributed, or transmitted in any form or by any means, including photocopying, recording, or other electronic or mechanical methods, without the prior written permission of the publisher, except in the case of brief quotations embodied in critical reviews and certain other noncommercial uses permitted by copyright law

Table of contents

Introduction

Montenegro, a tiny Balkan nation with rocky mountains, historic settlements, and a long length of Adriatic coastline, provides an unforgettable experience. My voyage through this hidden jewel was nothing short of unforgettable, with interactions that combined nature's raw beauty, the deep pulse of history, and the friendliness of its people.

I came to Montenegro full of excitement, hoping to discover the country's best-hidden secret. Despite being overshadowed by more prominent neighbors such as Croatia and Greece, Montenegro stands out as a destination of great natural beauty and cultural depth. My first visit was to the Bay of Kotor, which is a UNESCO World Heritage Site and one of Europe's most stunning natural settings. As I dropped into the bay, I was impressed by its sheer grandeur—steep limestone cliffs towering above the deep blue seas, punctuated by attractive tiny villages like Perast and Kotor itself.

Kotor, a medieval village on the bay's edge, is ringed by well-preserved city walls that rise from the slopes. As I meandered through its winding lanes, I felt transported back in time. The stone houses, churches, and tiny lanes lent an air of mystery and intrigue. One of the pleasures of my trip to Kotor was ascending the 1,350 stairs to the top of the city walls. The view from the stronghold was breathtaking—a wide panorama of the water, mountains, and town below. The sensation of success after the long ascent made the experience even more memorable.

Montenegro's coastline appeal goes beyond Kotor. I traveled to Budva, one of the country's most popular tourist destinations. Budva, known for its magnificent beaches, active nightlife, and ancient old town, provided a distinct contrast to Kotor. Budva's old town is a tangle of cobblestone lanes and historic stone buildings, similar to Kotor's, but with a more laid-back, beachy vibe. I spent my days relaxing on the golden beaches, swimming in the crystal-clear seas, and visiting the old town's cafés, shops, and restaurants. One evening, I went to a local performance of traditional Montenegrin music and dancing. The energetic rhythms, mixed with the stunning coastline setting, created a spectacular experience that deepened my understanding of the local culture.

Another highlight of my trip to Montenegro was seeing the island of Sveti Stefan. This distinctive islet, linked to the mainland by a thin causeway, is now a luxury resort, but its origins as a walled hamlet date back to the fifteenth century. I did not stay on the island, but I spent hours admiring its distinctive architecture and tranquil beauty from adjacent beaches. The sunset views over Sveti Stefan were among the most unforgettable parts of my trip—the fiery orange sky reflected on the calm seas, with the island's outline standing strongly against the background.

While Montenegro's shoreline is gorgeous, the country's interior is just as intriguing. I traveled inland to see Durmitor National Park, a UNESCO-listed natural treasure in the country's north. Towering peaks, deep valleys, and glacial lakes are among the park's most striking features. Hiking through Durmitor was one of the most memorable experiences I had while in Montenegro. The routes led me through thick pine woods, high-altitude meadows, and along the brink of precipitous cliffs. The hike's highlight was reaching Black Lake, a beautiful glacial lake surrounded by mountains. The lake was so clean and quiet that the neighboring peaks seemed perfectly mirrored on the surface. I sat by the lake for what seemed like hours, soaking in the tranquility and beauty of the surroundings.

Durmitor National Park also includes Montenegro's Tara River Canyon, which is the world's second-deepest canyon after the Grand Canyon. I opted to explore the canyon in the most exhilarating manner possible: rafting down the Tara River. The experience was exciting. While navigating the river's rapids, I was surrounded by high cliffs, lush trees, and waterfalls falling down canyon walls. It was an exhilarating journey that contrasted well with the peaceful and tranquil times I had experienced elsewhere in the nation.

Of course, no vacation to Montenegro is complete without tasting the country's cuisine and friendliness. Montenegrin cuisine combines Mediterranean and Balkan influences, with a focus on fresh, local ingredients. I ate great seafood along the shore, especially grilled fish and octopus, complemented by local wines. In the hilly areas, I appreciated heavy foods like "kačamak" (a typical Montenegrin dish with potatoes, cheese, and cream) and smoked meats. Everywhere I went, I was greeted warmly. The residents were eager to share their tales, customs, and cuisine with me, making my stay in Montenegro even more enjoyable.

When I think back on my stay in Montenegro, the most memorable aspect is the tremendous variety of activities available. From the ancient villages along the coast to the rough wildness of the highlands, Montenegro has something fresh and stunning around every bend. It's a nation that encourages exploration, whether you're searching for adventure, leisure, or a thorough understanding of history and culture.

My stay in Montenegro was amazing, and I developed a profound respect for the country's distinct character. Montenegro may be tiny, but its beauty, history, and culture make it a destination that well outperforms its size. It's a spot I'll remember fondly for years to come, and I'm certain I'll want to return in the future.

Why should you visit Montenegro?

Montenegro, a hidden jewel in the Balkans, seamlessly combines natural beauty and ancient history. This little yet powerful nation has a varied selection of experiences to suit every sort of tourist. Montenegro offers something for everyone, whether you want to go on an adventure, learn about history, or relax by the sea.

First and foremost, the vistas are breathtaking. Consider this: towering mountains that seem to reach the sky, gorgeous beaches with crystal-clear seas, and lush woods ideal for trekking. Durmitor National Park is a must-see destination for wildlife aficionados. It is home to the Tara River Canyon, one of Europe's deepest gorges, which provides exhilarating rafting adventures and stunning scenery.

The beach village of Kotor is another standout. Kotor's historic old town, located amid towering mountains and the Adriatic Sea, is a UNESCO World Heritage site. Wander through its small, cobblestone alleyways, see historic churches, and climb the city walls to get a panoramic view of the bay. The Bay of Kotor is sometimes likened to a fjord due to its spectacular landscape and calm seas.

Montenegro's beaches are equally appealing. From the busy beaches of Budva to the calm shores of Sveti Stefan, there is something for everyone who enjoys the beach. Budva is famous for its lively nightlife and ancient old town, whilst Sveti Stefan provides a more intimate experience with its luxury resorts and private beaches.

Montenegro is a must-see for history and culture enthusiasts. Perast, with its baroque architecture and island chapels, offers a glimpse into the past. Meanwhile, Podgorica, the capital city, combines modernism with history with museums, galleries, and a vibrant café culture.

Foodies can also find plenty to enjoy in Montenegro. The food here is a delicious fusion of Mediterranean and Balkan tastes. Fresh fish, substantial meats, and locally produced veggies are commonplace. Don't miss eating local favorites like Njeguški pršut (smoked ham) and Kacamak (a traditional potato and cheese dish).

Montenegro is also a hotspot for adventure sports. There are plenty of adrenaline-pumping activities to choose from, like hiking in the mountains, riding along gorgeous paths, and zip-lining over valleys. The country's small size allows you to effortlessly transition from alpine activities to beach leisure in a single day.

Montenegro's Climate and Geography

Montenegro's climate and landscape are both unique and intriguing. This little Balkan country delivers a punch with its diverse landscapes and weather patterns, making it a year-round tourist attraction.

Beginning with the shore, Montenegro has a Mediterranean climate. Summers here are hot and dry, ideal for beachgoers eager to soak up the rays. Coastal communities like Budva and Kotor have temperatures that often exceed 30°C (86°F) during the peak summer months. Winters, on the other hand, are pleasant and moist, with temperatures never falling below 10°C (50°F). This makes the seaside area a delightful retreat even during the winter months.

The environment changes considerably as you get farther inland. The middle and northern regions of Montenegro have a more continental climate. Summers are still mild, but winters may be cold, with significant snowfall turning the scenery into a winter wonderland. The mountainous areas, notably Durmitor and Bjelasica, are well-known for their frigid winters, making them perfect for winter sports aficionados.

Geographically, Montenegro is a country of contrasts. The coastal plain is tiny, generally just a few kilometers broad, yet it swiftly transitions to rocky mountains. The Bay of Kotor, which is sometimes mistaken for a fjord, is a breathtaking example of Montenegro's spectacular coastline environment. This harbor, surrounded by rugged mountains, is one of the most attractive in the nation.

Inland, the landscape becomes considerably more diverse. The Dinaric Alps dominate the scene, with peaks reaching above 2,000 meters (6,562 feet). Durmitor National Park, a UNESCO World Heritage site, has some of Europe's highest peaks and deepest gorges. The Tara River Canyon, for example, is the world's second deepest, with spectacular vistas and exhilarating rafting chances.

Montenegro's karst terrain is yet another geographical gem. Sinkholes, caverns, and subterranean rivers are common features in this limestone terrain. Examples of this topography include the Zeta River Valley and the Bjelopavlići Plain, which are heavily inhabited and ideal for agriculture.

Lake Skadar, the biggest lake in the Balkans, is on the boundary between Montenegro and Albania. This freshwater lake is a shelter for animals, especially bird species, and provides a peaceful retreat for nature enthusiasts. The adjacent wetlands and marshes provide a sharp contrast to the steep mountains and coastal cliffs.

Accommodation Options

Montenegro has a variety of lodging alternatives to meet any traveler's requirements and budget. From opulent beachfront resorts to lovely boutique hotels and low-cost hostels, you'll discover a location that feels perfect.

For those looking for luxury, the beach village of Sveti Stefan is an excellent alternative. The Aman Sveti Stefan, situated on a lovely islet, provides a special experience with its beautifully renovated stone villas and breathtaking sea views. The address is Sveti Stefan, 85315, Montenegro. This resort is ideal for anyone seeking for some pampering, with private beaches, a world-class spa, and great dining choices.

The Avala Resort & Villas in Budva is a popular choice. Situated in Mediteranska br. This resort, located at 2, 85310 Budva, Montenegro, offers contemporary facilities as well as a beautiful beachfront position. Guests will appreciate the large accommodations, various swimming pools, and convenient proximity to Budva's bustling nightlife and historic old town.

The Palazzo Radomiri Hotel in Kotor offers a more personal experience. This boutique hotel, situated at Dobrota 220, 85330 Kotor, Montenegro, is housed in a refurbished 18th-century mansion. With its exquisite accommodations, waterfront patio, and individualized service, it's ideal for a romantic trip. The hotel's position also makes it convenient to see Kotor's picturesque old town and the breathtaking Bay of Kotor.

Budget-conscious travelers can also find lots of alternatives. The Old Town Hostel in Kotor, situated at Stari Grad 284, 85330 Kotor, Montenegro, provides an economical dormitory and individual rooms in a historic structure. It's an excellent spot to meet other tourists and discover the neighborhood, thanks to its welcoming environment, common kitchen, and scheduled events.

In Podgorica, the capital city, the Hotel Aurel provides a nice stay without breaking the budget. This contemporary hotel, located at Bulevar Josipa Broza Tita bb, 81000 Podgorica, Montenegro, has large rooms, a fitness facility, and a rooftop terrace with spectacular city views. It is strategically located in the city center, making it simple to visit Podgorica's attractions and food establishments.

For those seeking a more rural experience, the Eco Resort Cermeniza near Virpazar is an excellent alternative. Nestled in the heart of Montenegro's wine region, this eco-friendly resort provides small cottages in a tranquil location surrounded by vineyards and wildlife. The location is: Virpazar bb, 81305 Virpazar, Montenegro. Guests may participate in wine tastings, farm-to-table meals, and outdoor activities like hiking and bird viewing.

1-week itinerary

Day 1: Arrival in Kotor

Begin your tour at the historic village of Kotor, which sits on a harbor surrounded by high limestone cliffs. Wander through the intricate alleyways of the Old Town, a UNESCO World Heritage site, where every corner has a piece of history. Climb the medieval city walls to get a panoramic view of the harbor, and don't miss the Cathedral of Saint Tryphon, a Romanesque architectural wonder. In the evening, dine at one of the local konobas (taverns) and sample fresh seafood and Montenegrin wine.

Day 2 - Perast and Our Lady of the Rocks

A short drive from Kotor takes you to the lovely village of Perast. This lovely hamlet is renowned for its baroque mansions and churches. Take a boat to Our Lady of the Rocks, a man-made island where you may see the seafarers' chapel and museum. Spend the day exploring Perast's tiny alleyways and seaside cafés before returning to Kotor for the night.

Day 3: Lovćen National Park & Cetinje.

Explore Lovćen National Park, which includes the tomb of Montenegro's poet and king, Petar II Petrović-Njegoš. The trip up the serpentine road provides stunning views of the Bay of Kotor. After touring the tomb, go to Cetinje, the former royal capital. Explore the National Museum of Montenegro and the old Cetinje Monastery. Return to Kotor in the evening.

Day 4: Budva & Sveti Stefan

Travel down the coast to Budva, which is famed for its vibrant atmosphere and stunning beaches. Stroll around the Old Town, which has Venetian walls and small lanes. After basking in the sun on Mogren Beach, go to the renowned islet of Sveti Stefan. Although the island is now a luxury resort, you may still appreciate its beauty from the mainland and take a dip at the neighboring beach. Stay the night in Budva.

Day 5: Lake Skadar

Visit Lake Skadar, the biggest lake in the Balkans and a sanctuary for birdwatchers. Take a boat cruise to see the tranquil waterways, which are studded with lily pads and surrounded by mountains. Visit the picturesque town of Virpazar to savor local wines and fresh seafood. If you're feeling daring, go up to the Besac fortification for breathtaking views of the lake. Return to Budva for the night.

Day 6 - Durmitor National Park

Set off early for Durmitor National Park, a UNESCO World Heritage site renowned for its spectacular scenery. The route leads you into the Tara River Canyon, which is one of Europe's deepest. In the park, you may climb to Black Lake, which is bordered by lush pine trees and tall hills. For the most daring, consider rafting on the Tara River. Spend a night in the highland town of Žabljak.

Day 7: Podgorica & Departure

On your last day, visit Montenegro's capital, Podgorica. While not as charming as the beach towns, it provides an insight into contemporary Montenegrin life. Explore the Millennium Bridge, the Orthodox Cathedral of Christ's Resurrection, and the remains of Doclea, an old Roman city. Before you go, have a leisurely lunch at one of the city's cafés and reflect on your week's activities.

The best time to visit

Montenegro is a place that shines year-round, but the ideal time to visit depends on your preferences. This little Balkan country has a range of temperatures and activities throughout the year, making it an adaptable destination for tourists.

Spring, from April to June, is an excellent season to visit Montenegro. The weather is pleasant, with temperatures ranging from 15°C to 25°C (59°F to 77°F), ideal for outdoor activities like hiking and sightseeing. The sceneries are lush and green, with wildflowers in full bloom. This is also an excellent season to explore national parks like Durmitor and Biogradska Gora, where you can appreciate the natural splendor without the summer throng.

Summer, from July to August, is the major tourist season. The seaside regions, like as Budva, Kotor, and Sveti Stefan, are crowded with tourists enjoying the Mediterranean environment. Temperatures may reach 30°C (86°F) and higher, making it excellent for beachgoers. The Adriatic Sea is warm and welcoming, ideal for swimming, sailing, and other water activities. However, be prepared for overcrowded beaches and increased costs during this period.

Autumn, from September to October, is another great season to come. The weather remains pleasant, particularly around the shore, but summer tourists have thinned out. This is an excellent time to explore the old towns and sample the local food. Vineyards are also in harvest, making it an ideal time for wine-tasting trips in areas such as Lake Skadar.

Montenegro has a certain appeal throughout the winter season, which lasts from November to March. The coastal parts are calmer, with temperatures hovering around 10°C (50°F), making it a relaxing refuge. Meanwhile, the mountainous areas turn into a winter paradise. Ski resorts such as Kolašin and Žabljak provide exceptional skiing and snowboarding experiences. The holiday season includes Christmas markets and traditional festivals, which lend a wonderful touch to your stay.

Getting to Montenegro

International Airports and Flights

Montenegro, a jewel on the Adriatic coast, is serviced by two major international airports: Podgorica and Tivat. These portals offer your first introduction to a nation of breathtaking scenery, rich history, and lively culture.

Podgorica Airport is situated in the center of Montenegro, giving it an ideal starting point for seeing the whole nation.

The airport is about 30 minutes from the coast and an hour from the closest mountain destinations. This strategic position allows you to conveniently travel from the busy metropolis to tranquil beaches or rough mountains. Podgorica Airport handles a wide range of international flights, linking Montenegro to many European cities. The airport itself is contemporary and efficient, with everything you may need, from vehicle rentals to eateries.

If you're traveling directly toward the seaside, however, Tivat Airport is your best bet. Tivat Airport, located on the gorgeous Boka Bay, is ideal for visitors wishing to experience Montenegro's coastal beauty straight immediately. The airport is smaller than Podgorica but just as essential, particularly during the summer months when visitors swarm to the Adriatic coast. Tivat is connected to numerous major European centers, making it simple to obtain direct flights from many locations.

For those looking for a bigger experience, Dubrovnik Airport in Croatia is just a short drive from the Montenegrin border. This option is especially beneficial if you intend to visit both Montenegro and Croatia. Dubrovnik Airport has a large selection of foreign flights, allowing you to arrange your trip with flexibility and ease.

Visa and Entry Requirements

Planning a vacation to Montenegro? Here's all you need to know about visas and entrance criteria to have a pleasant trip.

Montenegro's admission procedures are reasonably easy, making it an appealing destination for tourists. Citizens of the European Union, the United States, Canada, Australia, and many other countries are permitted to visit Montenegro without a visa for stays of up to 90 days within a 180-day window. This visa-free access is part of Montenegro's efforts to enhance tourism and make travel more convenient for tourists.

If you are from a nation that needs a visa, the procedure is straightforward. You may apply for a visa at your local Montenegrin embassy or consulate. The application usually involves a completed form, a valid passport, a current picture, proof of travel insurance, and proof of adequate finances for your stay. It is always a good idea to check the Montenegrin government website or contact the embassy directly for the most up-to-date requirements since restrictions sometimes change.

If you want to remain for more than 90 days, whether for job, school, or other reasons, you must apply for a temporary residence visa. This procedure requires extra evidence, such as a letter of invitation, verification of accommodations, and, in certain cases, a background check. These applications are handled by the local police station in Montenegro, and it is recommended that you begin the procedure well in advance of your planned stay.

Upon arriving in Montenegro, ensure that your passport is stamped at the border. This stamp is important since it signals the start of your authorized stay. If you are coming by land, particularly from adjacent countries such as Croatia or Serbia, be sure that border authorities stamp your passport. Failure to do so may result in issues when you leave the country.

Montenegro participates in the Schengen Area's visa-free system but is not a Schengen member. This implies that your stay in Montenegro will not count against your Schengen Zone 90-day restriction. This might be very handy for those who want to prolong their European journey without overstaying their Schengen visa.

Local Transportation Options

Montenegro's transportation choices appeal to a wide range of travel preferences and costs, making it easy to navigate. Whether you're touring the seaside cities or heading into the hilly interior, getting around is simple and frequently quite picturesque.

Buses are the primary mode of public transportation in Montenegro. They link large cities like Podgorica, Kotor, and

Budva to smaller towns and villages. The bus network is broad and dependable, with regular service that makes it simple to go from one location to another. Tickets are inexpensive and may be purchased at bus terminals or straight from the driver. The buses themselves vary from contemporary coaches to more rudimentary vehicles, but they all perform the job. Check schedules ahead of time for the greatest experience, particularly if you're visiting less popular destinations.

Trains provide a one-of-a-kind method to see the nation at a slower pace. The primary railway line connects Bar on the coast with Bijelo Polje in the north, passing via Podgorica. This path is noted for its breathtaking vistas, particularly as it weaves over the highlands. While rail service is less regular than bus service, it is a more pleasant and picturesque choice, especially for people who want to travel slowly.

Taxis are extensively accessible and reasonably priced compared to Western Europe. They are a useful choice for short excursions inside cities or to places that are not well-serviced by public transportation. To prevent overcharging, utilize licensed cabs or applications such as Taxi Montenegro. Always check the meter or agree on a fee before beginning your trip.

Car rentals are popular among individuals who seek greater freedom. Renting a vehicle allows you to explore at your leisure and visit more isolated locations. Montenegro's roads are typically in decent condition, however, some mountain routes are small and twisting. Driving down the shore provides breathtaking vistas, but be prepared for traffic in the summer months. Most major automobile rental companies operate in Montenegro, and vehicles may be picked up at airports or in bigger cities.

In coastal places, ferries and water taxis provide a picturesque alternative to transportation. These services are especially handy for visiting the Bay of Kotor and the many islands and peninsulas that line the shore. Ferries travel frequently between significant destinations, and water taxis may be booked for more customized excursions.

Finally, for the environmentally concerned visitor, cycling is becoming more popular in Montenegro. The nation has several bicycle routes, ranging from easy beach walks to tough mountain treks. Many municipalities have bike rental businesses, and some hotels provide bicycles to their visitors.

Drive in Montenegro.

Driving across Montenegro is an experience that combines breathtaking beach scenery with winding mountain roads. Whether you're planning a leisurely drive along the Adriatic coast or a more adventurous trip into the interior, here's all you need to know about Montenegro's roads, tolls, and car rentals.

Montenegro's road network is typically in excellent shape, with major roads being well-maintained and correctly marked. The E65/E80 coastal route connects the Croatian border in the north to the Albanian border in the south, passing through important cities such as Kotor, Budva, and Bar. This road has stunning views of the Adriatic Sea and is a must-drive for anybody visiting the nation. Inland, roads might be smaller and more twisting, particularly as you approach hilly areas. The trip from Podgorica to Kolašin offers breathtaking scenery.

One of the advantages of driving in Montenegro is the absence of toll roads. You won't have to stop to pay tolls, making your travel go more smoothly. However, there is a fee for utilizing the Sozina Tunnel, which links the capital, Podgorica, to the seaside resort of Bar. This tunnel considerably lowers travel time between the shore and the interior, making it an attractive alternative despite the low cost.

When it comes to automobile rentals, there are lots of possibilities at Podgorica and Tivat airports, as well as significant towns and cities. International rental businesses such as Hertz and Avis work alongside local enterprises, providing you with a variety of options. It is recommended that you reserve your rental vehicle in advance, particularly during the peak summer months when demand is strong. Most rental vehicles in Montenegro are manual, so be sure you request an automatic when reserving.

Driving in Montenegro needs a valid driver's license from your home country. If your license does not use the Latin alphabet, you may additionally require an International Driving Permit. The regulations of the road are the same as in other European countries: drive on the right, overtake on the left, and always wear your seatbelt. Headlights must be turned on at all times, even during the day, and using a mobile phone while driving is illegal unless you have a hands-free system.

Parking may be difficult in the busier tourist destinations, particularly during the summer. Parking places in locations like Kotor and Budva are scarce and may rapidly fill up. Look for dedicated parking lots or garages, and expect to pay for parking in these places. Parking is simpler to come by in smaller cities and rural locations, and it is typically free.

Fuel stations are widespread across Montenegro, with the majority supplying both unleaded gasoline and diesel. Credit cards are generally accepted, but it's always a good idea to bring extra cash, particularly if you're going to a distant location.

Must-See Attractions

Podgorica

Podgorica, Montenegro's capital, may not be the first place that springs to mind when planning a European journey, but it's a hidden gem that should be explored. This city, situated between the Dinaric Alps and the Adriatic Sea, combines history, culture, and natural beauty. Here's a list of the top attractions you shouldn't miss.

Begin your tour at Saborni Hram Hristovog Vaskrsenja, widely known as the Cathedral of the Resurrection of Christ. This spectacular Serbian Orthodox church, finished in 2013, is a contemporary architectural wonder, with exquisite paintings and a grandiose design. It is open every day from 7 a.m. to 8 p.m. and is free to enter.

Next, see the Millennium Bridge, Podgorica's distinctive emblem. This cable-stayed bridge across the Morača River provides stunning views of the city and is ideal for a relaxing walk, particularly around dusk. It is strategically positioned, allowing you to easily combine your visit with other surrounding sites.

For a taste of nature, go to Gorica Hill, which is popular with both residents and visitors. This grassy haven in the center of the city is ideal for hiking, riding, or just resting. The park is open all day, every day, and there is no entrance cost. Don't miss the Partisan Memorial, a moving reminder of Montenegro's past during WWII.

The Ribnica Bridge, commonly known as Adži-paša's Bridge, is another must-see attraction. At the junction of the Ribnica and Morača rivers, there is a historic stone bridge from Roman times. It's a lovely location for photography and a peaceful area to ponder on the city's history.

If you're interested in history, the Podgorica City Museum has a wealth of relics and displays. The museum, located at Marka

Miljanova 4, is open Monday through Friday from 9 a.m. to 5 p.m. and Saturdays from 10 a.m. to 2 p. Admission costs roughly €2 for adults and €1 for youngsters.

The Niagara Waterfalls on the Cijevna River provide a one-of-a-kind experience. These waterfalls are a short drive from the city center and provide a peaceful respite from the daily bustle. There's a tiny café nearby where you may sip a drink while admiring the scenery. The greatest time to visit is in the spring when the water flow is at its highest.

Don't miss Stara Varoš (Old Town), a historic district that reflects Podgorica's Ottoman heritage. Wander through its tiny alleyways, see the antique clock tower, and dine at one of the classic eateries. It's the ideal way to conclude your day in Podgorica.

Kotor

Kotor, a beach town in Montenegro, combines history and natural beauty harmoniously. This lovely village, set in the Bay of Kotor, provides a diverse range of activities for visitors. Here's a list of some of the best attractions to visit.

Begin your journey at the Old Town of Kotor, a UNESCO World Heritage site. This well-preserved medieval town is a tangle of small alleys, squares, and historical structures. As you go through, you'll come to the Cathedral of Saint Tryphon, a majestic Romanesque structure that dates back to 1166. Located on Trg Sv. Tripuna's cathedral is open every day from 8 a.m. to 8 p.m., with a €2 admission charge.

Next, go to the Maritime Museum, which is situated in a stunning Baroque palace. This museum provides an intriguing view into Kotor's maritime history, with displays ranging from miniature ships to navigational tools. It is located at Trg Bokeljske Mornarice 391 and is open weekdays from 9 AM to

8 PM and weekends from 10 AM to 4 PM. Admission costs €4 for adults and €1 for youngsters.

Hiking up to the Kotor Fortress provides spectacular views. The ascent is tough, but the panoramic views of the harbor and town below are well worth the effort. The stronghold is accessible from the Old Town, and it is recommended to begin early in the morning to escape the noon sun. The entry price is €8, and it is open from 8 a.m. to 8 p.m.

Don't miss the Church of St. Luke, a modest yet attractive church dating back to 1195. It is situated on Trg Sv. Luke is open every day from 8 a.m. until 8 p.m. Entry is free, and the church's basic but magnificent interior provides a calm respite from the busy streets outside.

The Cat Museum offers a unique experience. Yes, you read it correctly! Kotor features a cat museum, which reflects the town's affection for these cuddly animals. The museum is situated at Kotor Stari Grad 371, and is open from 10 a.m. to 6 p.m. Admission is €1.

After seeing the town, take a boat ride to Our Lady of the Rocks, a man-made island with a beautiful chapel and museum. Boats leave from the Kotor marina on a regular basis, with the journey costing around €5. The island is available for guests from 9 a.m. to 7 p.m.

Finally, relax at one of the numerous cafés and restaurants in the Old Town. Try local delights like Njeguški pršut (smoked ham) and Kotor's well-known seafood dishes. The town's thriving nightlife provides lots of opportunities for a peaceful evening.

Budva

Budva, a treasure on Montenegro's Adriatic coast, seamlessly combines old heritage with dynamic modernity. Budva is a must-see destination due to its beautiful beaches, vibrant nightlife, and rich cultural history. Here's a list of some of the best sights to see.

Begin your adventure at the Old Town (Stari Grad), a stunningly preserved medieval walled city. Wander through its tiny cobblestone alleyways to see attractive squares, antique churches, and little businesses. The Old Town is home to the Citadel, a stronghold with panoramic views of the Adriatic Sea. The Citadel at Stari Grad is open every day from 9 a.m. to 8 p.m., with a €2 admission charge.

Next, visit Mogren Beach, one of Budva's most popular beaches. This sandy length is broken into two sections, joined by a tunnel through the cliffs. It's an ideal location for sunbathing, swimming, and admiring the gorgeous blue seas.

Mogren Beach is just a short walk from the Old Town and is open all day with no entrance cost.

For a sense of local history, go to the Church of St. John, a stunning 7th-century church in the center of the Old Town. The church's bell tower provides spectacular views of Budva and the surrounding surroundings. It is open every day from 8 a.m. to 8 p.m., and admission is free.

Another must-see is Jaz Beach, a busy cove noted for its dynamic ambiance and music events, including the renowned Sea Dance Festival. Jaz Beach is situated around 2.5 kilometers from Budva and may be accessed by vehicle or bus. The beach is accessible all day and there is no entrance cost.

The Budva City Museum offers a one-of-a-kind experience by displaying objects from Budva's rich past, including Roman and Byzantine relics. The museum, situated at Petra I Petrovića, is open from 9 AM to 5 PM on weekdays and 10

AM to 2 PM on Saturdays. Admission costs €2 for adults and €1 for youngsters.

If you're searching for some adventure, take a boat excursion to Sveti Nikola Island, often known as Hawaii. This island is just a short boat trip from Budva and provides gorgeous beaches, crystal-clear seas, and a calm getaway from the busy city. Boats leave from the Budva marina on a regular basis, with the journey costing around €5.

Finally, don't miss the opportunity to visit Slovenska Plaza, a major seaside resort area with several restaurants, cafés, and stores. It's a terrific location to unwind, dine, and take up the vibrant environment. The resort is open all day and there is no entrance cost.

Hercegov Novi

Herceg Novi, a lovely town on Montenegro's Adriatic coast, offers a wealth of history, culture, and natural beauty. Herceg Novi, known for its picturesque old town, gorgeous fortifications, and pleasant beaches, provides visitors with a fascinating variety of activities. Here's a list of some of the best attractions to visit.

Begin your trip in the Old Town (Stari Grad), a maze of small alleyways, stone homes, and bustling squares. The Church of St. Michael the Archangel is located in Belavista Square, which serves as the core of the Old Town. This 19th-century chapel, made of Korčula stone, is a peaceful place to begin the day. The church is open every day from 8 a.m. to 8 p.m., and admission is free.

Next, see the Clock Tower (Sahat Kula), an Ottoman relic erected in 1667. The tower, which was previously an entry gate to the town, provides a look into Herceg Novi's history. It is situated in the Old Town and is open all day with no admission fees.

Kanli Kula, a 16th-century stronghold with breathtaking vistas, is a must-see for history buffs. Perched high above the village, this fortification provides panoramic views of the Bay of Kotor. It is open every day from 9 a.m. to 8 p.m., with a €2 admission charge. During the summer, Kanli Kula organizes a variety of cultural events and concerts, which add to its appeal.

Another must-see is the Forte Mare, a beach castle constructed by Bosnian King Tvrtko I in 1382. This stronghold, situated at the entrance to the Bay of Kotor, is ideal for a stroll and provides beautiful views of the Adriatic. It is open every day from 9 a.m. to 8 p.m., with a €2 admission charge.

For a more spiritual experience, visit the Savina Monastery, a stunning structure dating back to the 11th century. Nestled amid lush vegetation, the monastery, which comprises three churches, provides a calm respite from the hustle and bustle of town. It is open from 8 a.m. to 6 p.m. on weekdays and 8 a.m. to 12 p.m. on Sundays. Entry is free, however contributions are welcome.

If you want to relax by the sea, go to Igalo Beach, which is famed for its medicinal mud and mineral springs. This beach is popular among both residents and visitors, with a variety of services such as cafés, restaurants, and water sports. It's open all day and there's no admission price.

A boat ride to the Blue Cave, a breathtaking natural grotto on the Lustica Peninsula, provides a one-of-a-kind experience. The cave is noted for its stunning blue waters, which are lit by sunshine. Boat cruises leave from the Herceg Novi marina regularly, with prices starting at about €20.

Finally, don't miss the opportunity to walk along the Pet Danica Promenade, a 7-kilometer-long boardwalk that runs down the coast from Igalo to Meljine. This picturesque promenade is dotted with cafés, restaurants, and stores, making it an ideal spot to relax and enjoy the scenery.

Cetinje

Cetinje, Montenegro's ancient core, is a town full of beauty and character. Located at the foot of Mount Lovćen, this old royal capital has several cultural and historical attractions. Here's a list of some of the best attractions to visit.

Begin your adventure in the Cetinje Monastery, a spiritual and cultural center dating back to the fifteenth century. This monastery, situated on Ulica Baja Pivljanina, has rare relics, including St. John the Baptist's right hand. It is open every day from 8 a.m. to 6 p.m., and admission is free, but donations are welcome.

Next, go to the National Museum of Montenegro, which is a group of museums located in historical structures. The King Nikola's Palace, at Njegoševa 28, is a highlight. This historic royal house provides insight into the life of Montenegro's last monarch. The museum is open Monday through Friday from 9 a.m. to 5 p.m., and Saturday and Sunday from 10 a.m. Admission costs €5 for adults and €2 for youngsters.

Exploring the Biljarda, also known as the Billiard House, will provide you with a unique experience. This was the home of Petar II Petrović-Njegoš, a renowned Montenegrin prince and poet. The building at Njegoševa 21 has a billiard table that Njegoš personally used. It is open every day from 9 a.m. to 5 p.m., with a €3 admission charge.

Don't miss the Blue Palace, the President of Montenegro's official house. While the palace is not available to the public, the spectacular blue façade and lovely grounds are worth seeing. It is situated at Njegoševa 10 and may be admired from outside at any time of day.

Lovćen National Park is a short drive from Cetinje and offers a natural experience. The park has the Mausoleum of Njegoš, a massive mausoleum of Petar II Petrović-Njegoš located on Mount Lovćen. The park is open every day from 8 a.m. to 8 p.m., with a €2 admission charge. The trek to the tomb is 461 steps long, but the panoramic views from the top are stunning.

Another must-see is Lipa Cave, one of Montenegro's biggest caverns. This cave, located approximately 5 kilometers from Cetinje, provides guided tours of its spectacular subterranean chambers. The cave is open from 10 a.m. to 6 p.m., with the tour costing €10 for adults and €5 for children.

Finally, meander around Cetinje's main plaza, Dvorski Trg, which is lined with cafés and stores, as well as the Royal Theatre Zetski Dom, Montenegro's oldest. The square is an ideal area to unwind and take in the town's laid-back vibe.

Nikšić

Nikšić, Montenegro's second biggest city, combines history, culture, and natural beauty. Nestled in a valley surrounded by mountains, this dynamic city has a plethora of activities for visitors. Here's a guide to some of the best places to visit.

Begin your journey with Slano Lake, an artificial lake popular among residents for its tranquil beauty and recreational activities. In the summer, the lake is ideal for a stroll, a picnic, or a refreshing swim. It's just a short drive from the city center and is open all day, with no admission price.

Next, visit Manitovac Park, a natural paradise in Nikšić. This park is perfect for families, with playgrounds, strolling routes, and a nice café where you can have coffee while the kids play. The park is open every day from 8 a.m. to 8 p.m., and admission is free.

For a taste of history, explore the church Church of St. Basil of Ostrog, a beautiful Orthodox church that dominates the city skyline. This church, situated on a hill in the heart of Nikšić, is a must-see for its stunning architecture and peaceful ambiance. It is open every day from 8 a.m. to 8 p.m., and admission is free.

Another historical landmark is the Bedem Fortress, which provides panoramic views of the city and neighboring mountains. This Ottoman-era castle is ideal for a stroll and spectacular picture possibilities. It's open all day and there's no admission price.

The Nikšić Heritage Museum showcases the city's rich history via artifacts and displays, making it a must-see for local culture enthusiasts. The museum, situated at Njegoševa 18, is open from 9 AM to 5 PM on weekdays and 10 AM to 2 PM on Saturdays. Admission costs €2 for adults and €1 for youngsters.

If you like nature, don't miss Krupac Lake, another stunning manmade lake situated just outside the city. This lake is a popular destination for fishermen, swimmers, and boaters. There are also various cafés and restaurants along the coast where you may unwind and enjoy the scenery. The lake is open all day with no admission price.

For a one-of-a-kind experience, go to the Ostrog Monastery, one of the most prominent Balkan pilgrimage destinations. This monastery, carved into a cliff face, provides breathtaking vistas and a serene environment. It is situated around 30 kilometers from Nikšić and is open every day from 6 AM to 6 PM. Entry is free, however contributions are welcome.

Finally, meander around the Freedom area, Nikšić's main area, where you'll discover cafés, stores, and the Nikšić Theatre, a cultural hotspot. The square is an ideal area to unwind and absorb the local ambiance.

Tivat

Tivat, a lovely seaside town in Montenegro, combines contemporary marina life with a rich past. Tivat, located on the Bay of Kotor, has a diverse range of attractions to suit everyone's preferences. Here's a guide to some of the best places to visit.

Begin your vacation in Porto Montenegro, a luxurious marina and residential complex that has converted Tivat into a fashionable tourist attraction. Stroll along the waterfront, view the superyachts, and visit the finest stores and restaurants. The marina is open all day, and although there is no admission charge, the pricing at the stores and restaurants may be rather costly.

Next, visit the Naval Heritage Collection in Porto Montenegro. This museum celebrates the region's maritime heritage via unique exhibits, including a reconstructed submarine. It is situated at Obala bb and is open every day from 9 a.m. to 9 p.m. The admission price is €5 for adults and €3 for children.

For a taste of nature, go to Big City Park, a rich green environment ideal for a stroll or picnic. The park is home to a variety of Mediterranean plants and trees, offering a peaceful respite from the busy waterfront. It is situated in the town center and is open all day with no admission price.

Another must-see is the Church of St. Sava, a stunning Orthodox church that embodies Tivat's cultural history. The church, situated at Trg Dara Petkovića, is open every day from 8 AM to 8 PM. Admission is free. Its tranquil interior and breathtaking frescoes make it an ideal hideaway.

A boat journey to Our Lady of Mercy Island provides a one-of-a-kind experience. This little island, right off the coast of Tivat, has a quaint chapel and wonderful views of the sea. Boats leave from the Tivat marina on a regular basis, with the journey costing around €5. The island is available for guests from 9 a.m. to 7 p.m.

If you adore the beach, Plavi Horizonti Beach is a must-see. This sandy beach, approximately 10 kilometers from Tivat, is famed for its crystal-clear blue seas and family-friendly ambiance. It's an ideal area for swimming, sunbathing, and water sports. The beach is accessible all day and there is no entrance cost.

The Buća-Luković Museum & Gallery, located in a medieval palace, offers a glimpse into local culture. This museum's collection of antiques and artworks provides an insight into Tivat's history. Located at Trg Dara Petkovića, it is open from 9 AM to 5 PM on weekdays and 10 AM to 2 PM on Saturdays. Admission costs €2 for adults and €1 for youngsters.

Finally, don't miss the opportunity to visit Gornja Lastva, a charming hamlet perched on a hill above Tivat. This settlement has amazing views of the sea and is an excellent site to experience traditional Montenegrin life. The town is open all day, and there is no admission cost.

Bar

Bar, a seaside town in Montenegro, offers a beautiful combination of history, culture, and natural beauty. This lesser-known treasure has a diverse range of activities to suit everyone's preferences. Here's a guide to some of the best places to visit.

Begin your adventure at Stari Bar (Old Bar), a unique landmark located around 4 kilometers from the current town core. This historic village, which dates back to roughly 800 BC, is a labyrinth of remains that depict the narrative of its Roman, Byzantine, Venetian, and Ottoman periods. The cobblestone walkways leading into the old town are dotted with attractive eateries and souvenir stores. The great entrance, embellished with Saint Mark's winged lion, welcomes you into a realm rich in history. Saint George's

Cathedral, Saint Nicholas Church, and the Turkish Bath are among the must-see attractions. Summer hours are 8 a.m. to 8 p.m., and winter hours are 9 a.m. to 5 p.m. Admission is €5 for adults and €1 for children aged 6 to 14.

Next, go to King Nikola's Palace, popularly known as the Homeland Museum. This beautiful mansion on the beachfront was completed in 1885 and currently serves as a museum, displaying relics from Bar's rich past. The palace is surrounded by stunning grounds, ideal for a leisurely walk. It is situated at Obala kralja Nikole and is open Monday through Friday from 9 a.m. to 5 p.m. and Saturday from 10 a.m. to 2 p. Admission costs €2 for adults and €1 for youngsters.

For a taste of local culture, visit the Church of St. Jovan Vladimir, a breathtaking Orthodox church that dominates the town's skyline. This new church, inaugurated in 2016, is renowned for its stunning design and peaceful environment. It is situated at Trg Vladimira i Kosare and is open every day from 8 a.m. to 8 p.m. Admission is free.

Another must-see is the Old Olive Tree, one of the world's oldest olive trees, thought to be more than 2,000 years old. This historic tree, which represents serenity and longevity, is situated in the Mirovica neighborhood, approximately 2 kilometers from the town center. The facility is accessible all day and charges a €1 admission fee.

The Bar Aqueduct, a magnificent structure erected in the 16th century to bring water to the ancient town, offers a one-of-a-kind experience. The aqueduct, with its 17 arches, demonstrates the engineering talents of the period. It is situated near Stari Bar and is open all day with no admission cost.

If you appreciate nature, don't miss Lake Skadar, the biggest lake in the Balkans and only a short drive from Bar. The lake is a refuge for birdwatchers and provides chances for boating, fishing, and bathing. Several travel companies in Bar provide day excursions to the lake, with rates beginning at about €20.

Relax at Šušanj Beach, a stunning pebble beach situated just north of the town center. This beach is renowned for its crystal-clear blue waves and family-friendly ambiance. It's an ideal location for swimming, sunbathing, and watching the sunset. The beach is accessible all day and there is no entrance cost.

Ulcinj

Ulcinj, a charming town on Montenegro's southern coast, combines history, culture, and natural beauty well. Ulcinj, known for its beautiful beaches, rich past, and active environment, provides visitors with a variety of activities. Here's a list of some of the best attractions to visit.

Begin your tour in the Old Town (Stari Grad), a historic city built on a hill overlooking the Adriatic Sea. This historic town, with its small cobblestone lanes and stone homes, is a pleasure to explore. Ulcinj Castle, with its panoramic views of the town and sea, is a must-see. The castle is open every day from 8 a.m. to 8 p.m., with an admission cost of €2. Don't miss the Museum of Ulcinj, which is housed inside the castle and displays the town's rich history via relics and exhibitions.

Head to Velika Plaža (Long Beach), a 13-kilometer expanse of sandy pleasure. This beach is ideal for sunbathing, swimming, and other water activities. It's simply a short drive from the town center and open all day with no admission price. Mala Plaža (Small Beach) offers a private experience with clean seas and a peaceful atmosphere.

Ada Bojana, a river island near the mouth of the Bojana River, offers a unique experience. This island is famed for its nude beach and relaxed environment. It's an excellent location for kite surfing, fishing, and eating fresh seafood at one of the island's several eateries. Ada Bojana is accessible by vehicle or boat, and there is no entrance charge.

Another must-see is Valdanos Bay, a picturesque inlet encircled by olive orchards. With its beautiful waters and picturesque vistas, this bay is ideal for a relaxing day at the beach. It is situated around 5 kilometers from Ulcinj and is open all day with no admission price.

Visit the Pasha's Mosque, Montenegro's oldest mosque, to get a sense of the local culture. This mosque, situated in the Old Town, is renowned for its stunning architecture and peaceful atmosphere. It is open every day from 8 a.m. to 8 p.m., and admission is free.

If you enjoy nature, visit Šasko Lake, a peaceful area around 15 kilometers from Ulcinj. This lake is a birdwatcher's paradise and provides chances for boating and fishing. The lake is open all day and there is no entrance charge.

Finally, go down the Ulcinj Promenade, a bustling waterfront area dotted with cafés, restaurants, and stores. This promenade is ideal for relaxing, eating, and taking in the town's bustling atmosphere. It's open all day and there's no admission price.

Pljevlja

Pljevlja, a lovely village in northern Montenegro, is a hidden treasure with a fascinating mix of history, culture, and natural beauty. Pljevlja, located in a valley surrounded by mountains, is an inviting site for exploration and discovery. Here's a list of some of the best attractions to visit.

Begin your tour in the Hussein-Pasha Mosque, a breathtaking specimen of Ottoman architecture. This mosque, built in the 16th century, is well-known for its ornate embellishments and stunning minarets. It is open every day from 8 a.m. to 8 p.m. on Ulica Kralja Petra in Pljevlja's center. Entry is free, however contributions are welcome.

Visit the Monastery of the Holy Trinity, one of Montenegro's most important religious monuments. This Serbian Orthodox monastery, dating back to the 13th century, is famous for its stunning paintings and peaceful atmosphere. It's open from 8 a.m. to 6 p.m. and free to enter.

For a taste of local history, visit the Pljevlja Heritage Museum, which houses relics from the town's rich history, including the Roman, Byzantine, and Ottoman eras. The museum is situated at Ulica Kralja Petra and is open from 9 a.m. to 5 p.m. on weekdays and 10 a.m. to 2 p. Admission costs €2 for adults and €1 for youngsters.

Another must-see is Municipium S, a historic Roman hamlet near Pljevlja. This archeological site provides a fascinating peek into the region's past via well-preserved ruins and informative exhibits. The facility is open every day from 8 a.m. to 6 p.m., and admission is free.

Tara Canyon, one of the world's deepest canyons, offers a one-of-a-kind experience. This natural treasure is ideal for adventurers, with options for rafting, trekking, and spectacular vistas. Several tour organizations in Pljevlja provide guided journeys to the canyon, with rates beginning from €50.

If you want to unwind, go to Vodice Park, a lovely green spot ideal for a leisurely walk or picnic. The park is situated in the town center and is accessible all day with no admission price. It's a terrific place to relax and take in the natural beauty of the surroundings.

Finally, don't miss out on exploring Pljevlja's Old Town, which is attractive with cobblestone lanes, traditional buildings, and historical sites. Wander around the old town, browse the local stores, and eat at one of the classic restaurants. It's the ideal way to conclude your day in Pljevlja.

Culture and Traditions

History of Montenegro

Montenegro, a hidden jewel in the Balkans, has a rich and diverse history to match its breathtaking scenery. This little country, with its craggy mountains and Adriatic coastline, has seen empires rise and fall, cultures conflict, and strong people emerge.

Our voyage starts in antiquity, with the Illyrians, the region's first known residents. These tribes, noted for their staunch independence, established the foundation for what would become Montenegro. By the 3rd century BC, the Illyrian monarchy had arisen, with its capital at Scutari (now Shkodër).

The Romans, ever the conquerors, came in the second century BC and included the territory of the province of Illyricum. Roman roads and fortresses continue to tell stories from this period, leaving an indelible stamp on the environment. Montenegro became part of the Eastern Roman Empire, often known as the Byzantine Empire when the Roman Empire divided. This time witnessed cultural mixing, with Roman and Illyrian customs merging to form a distinct Montenegrin identity.

Moving ahead to the Middle Ages, we find the emergence of Slavic states. By the ninth century, three principalities had emerged: Duklja in the south, Travunia in the west, and Rascia in the north. In 1042, Stefan Vojislav led Duklja to independence and established the Vojislavljević dynasty. Duklja flourished during this period, notably under Vojislav's son, Mihailo, and grandson, Bodin.

The name Montenegro, which means "Black Mountain," first appeared in the late 14th century, replacing the previous name Zeta. During this time, noble houses such as the Balšić and Crnojević steered through stormy regional politics and Ottoman expansion. By the 15th century, the majority of

Montenegro had come under Ottoman authority, although pockets of resistance persisted, notably in the mountainous areas.

From 1516 until 1852, Montenegro was controlled by prince-bishops, or vladikas, who held both spiritual and temporal power. This theocratic government contributed to maintaining Montenegrin autonomy and culture despite centuries of Ottoman control. The Petrović-Njegoš dynasty, which emerged in the late 17th century, played a major role in this time. Figures like Petar II Petrović-Njegoš left a lasting impact via government and literature.

The nineteenth century saw considerable developments. Montenegro progressively increased its territory and was recognized as an independent state by the Congress of Berlin in 1878. Montenegro existed as a kingdom briefly in the early twentieth century before being integrated into the newly established Kingdom of Serbs, Croats, and Slovenes (later Yugoslavia) in 1918.

During the tumultuous twentieth century, Montenegro saw the upheavals of World War II and the succeeding communist period under Yugoslavia. The disintegration of Yugoslavia in the 1990s created uncertainty, but Montenegro overcame these hurdles, proclaiming independence in 2006 after a vote.

Today, Montenegro is a symbol of persistence and flexibility, having withstood historical storms and emerged with a rich cultural tapestry. Its history is more than simply a sequence of events; it's a tale of people, places, and a resilient spirit. Whether you're roaming among ancient ruins, touring medieval monasteries, or just admiring the breathtaking scenery, Montenegro's history is ever-present, encouraging you to become a part of its continuous tale.

Montenegrin language and dialects

Montenegro, a region of spectacular scenery and rich cultural history, also has an intriguing linguistic tapestry. The Montenegrin language, legally recognized in 2007, reflects the country's distinct character and history.

Montenegrin is a Serbo-Croatian dialect having origins in Serbian, Croatian, and Bosnian. It is mostly based on the Shtokavian dialect, particularly the Eastern Herzegovinian variation. This dialect is the backbone of the language, giving it a recognizable but unique taste when compared to its linguistic kin.

One of the most fascinating elements of Montenegrin is the employment of both the Latin and Cyrillic alphabets. This dichotomy reflects the country's historical influences and location at the crossroads of East and West. While both scripts are taught in schools and used in official documents, the Latin alphabet is becoming more popular for daily usage.

The language has distinct phonetic subtleties that define it distinctive. Montenegrin has the sounds "ś" and "ź," which are not present in Serbian. These little changes may seem insignificant, yet they play an important part in the language's identity and speakers' feelings of pride.

Regional dialects in Montenegro complement the country's linguistic environment. The nation is split into two dialectal zones: the Eastern Herzegovinian dialect (west and northwest) and the Zeta-Raška dialect (east and southeast). Each location adds its flavor to the language, including differences in pronunciation, vocabulary, and even syntax.

In addition to Montenegrin, numerous more minority languages are legally recognized and spoken across the nation. Official languages of Montenegro include Albanian, Bosnian, Croatian, and Serbian, reflecting the country's broad ethnic composition. In locations with large minority populations, like Ulcinj and Pljevlja, bilingual signage and multilingual schooling are commonplace.

The Montenegrin language is more than simply a medium of communication; it is a living, changing representation of the country's tenacity and flexibility. Whether you're traversing the busy streets of Podgorica, visiting the ancient cities of Kotor and Cetinje, or climbing through the rocky mountains, the language you hear is an important component of Montenegro's cultural tapestry.

Festivals and Cultural event

Montenegro, with its magnificent Adriatic coastline and steep mountains, is both a visual feast and a cultural treasure trove. The country's festivals and cultural events showcase its rich tradition and dynamic energy.

One of the most anticipated events is the Kotor Carnival, which takes place in February or March. This festival turns the medieval town of Kotor into a vibrant display of color and music. The streets are filled with parades, masked parties, and performances, creating a joyous and fascinating ambiance. The carnival pays homage to Kotor's Venetian roots, combining tradition with contemporary pleasure.

In the summer, the Montenegro Film Festival in Herceg Novi attracts filmgoers from all around the world. This festival, held in July and August, features a varied spectrum of films, including local creations and international successes.

Screenings take place in gorgeous open-air locales, giving a magical element to the film experience.

Budva, renowned for its bustling nightlife, presents the Budva Theatre City Festival from July to August. This festival transforms the historic town into a stage, with acts ranging from classical plays to modern dance. The festival's diverse schedule guarantees that there is something for everyone, making it the cultural highlight of the summer.

August also brings Boka Nights in Boka Bay, a festivity that features a procession of lit boats. The celebration is visually stunning, with fireworks and music contributing to the joyous mood. It's the ideal combination of tradition and spectacle, attracting both residents and visitors.

For jazz fans, the Podgorica International Jazz Festival in November is a must-see. This event comprises performances by well-known jazz artists from throughout the globe, transforming the capital city into a hive of musical creation.

The tiny settings and impassioned performances make it an unforgettable experience for any music enthusiast.

Winter in Montenegro is distinguished by Christmas and New Year's celebrations, during which towns and cities are decked with lights and decorations. Markets pop up, selling local crafts and Christmas snacks, while music and plays add to the holiday spirit. It's a time of love and joy when communities come together in the spirit of the season.

Traditional Montenegrin Clothing and Music

Montenegro, with its spectacular scenery and rich cultural history, combines tradition and contemporary perfectly. This is particularly visible in its traditional attire and music, which provide a glimpse into the character of this Balkan country.

Traditional Montenegrin dress is a colorful reflection of the country's history and cultural influences. Men often wear a white shirt, a vest called a "džamadan," and a long coat called a "dolama." The outfit is finished with pants and a thick belt. The "kapa," a spherical hat with a black rim and a scarlet top, is the showpiece, frequently embellished with elaborate embroidery.

Women's traditional attire is also ornate. It generally includes a long, embroidered dress, an apron, and a vest. The clothing, which is often made of wool or cotton, is heavily embellished with vivid designs and gold thread. A headscarf or hat, known as a "kapa," is another frequent accessory. These clothing are not only for show; they reveal tales about the wearer's area, status, and even marital situation.

The artistry required in making these outfits is impressive. It might take months to produce a single costume, with workers diligently attending to every detail. This commitment to conserving ancient ways demonstrates the value of cultural heritage in Montenegro.

The music of Montenegro is as varied as its scenery. Traditional Montenegrin music has deep roots in the country's history and is distinguished by the usage of the "gusle," a single-stringed instrument played with a bow. The gusle is sometimes accompanied by epic poetry, or "epic songs," which tell stories of valor and historical events. These performances are more than simply entertainment; they are a method to preserve and pass along history to future generations.

Another prominent musical practice is the "kolo," a circle dance that is done at festivities and festivals. The dance is accompanied by energetic music performed on instruments such as accordion, tamburica, and flute. The kolo is a group activity that brings people together in a joyous display of solidarity and cultural pride.

Montenegro also has a strong heritage of vocal music. "Ojkanje" is a particular style of singing distinguished by a wailing sound. This kind of singing is often done by groups of men and is especially popular in rural regions. The songs generally address topics like love, nature, and everyday living.

In recent years, Montenegro has embraced current music forms, combining them with traditional components to produce a distinct sound. This mix is shown during festivals like Budva's Sea Dance Festival, which attracts both local and international performers.

Local Etiquette

Montenegro, with its breathtaking Adriatic shoreline and rocky mountains, is a country where tradition and modernity live together. Understanding local etiquette as you plan your trip can help you have a better time and connect with the kind Montenegrins.

First and foremost, welcomes in Montenegro combine formality and tenderness. When meeting someone for the first time, a strong handshake with direct eye contact is usual. Addressing persons by their titles, such as Mr., Mrs., or Miss, followed by their last name, demonstrates respect and appreciation, particularly in formal contexts. A warm embrace or a kiss on each cheek is customary among friends and relatives after getting to know them better.

Punctuality is important, so come on time for appointments and social functions. However, don't be shocked if your

Montenegrin hosts have a more casual attitude about time. It contributes to the region's relaxed atmosphere.

Montenegrins take their meals seriously. If you are welcomed to a local's house, it is usual to offer a little gift, such as flowers or a bottle of wine. Wait for the host to start eating before digging in. Complimenting the meal is always a nice idea since Montenegrins take pleasure in their culinary heritage.

Dress regulations in Montenegro vary based on the situation. People in metropolitan regions like Podgorica and seaside towns like Budva dress smartly while being informal. However, while visiting holy locations, modest clothing is essential. This involves covering your shoulders and knees. The dress code in rural places is more lenient, yet it is always advisable to dress appropriately.

Montenegrins are recognized for their hospitality, and you'll frequently be welcomed for a coffee or a meal. Accepting these invites is an excellent approach to having personal familiarity with the local culture. Coffee culture is very popular here, with cafes functioning as social gathering places where people can converse and relax.

When conversing, it is better to avoid sensitive issues like politics and religion until you know the individual well. Montenegrins take pride in their history and culture, thus expressing interest and asking polite questions about these issues may lead to meaningful talks.

Tipping is welcomed, but not required. In restaurants, a tip of around 10% is considered generous. It is a great gesture for taxi drivers and hotel workers to round up the cost or leave a tiny tip.

Finally, be conscious of your personal space. Montenegrins cherish their privacy and avoid unwanted inquiries or subjects. A warm approach and genuine interest in the local way of life will help you enjoy your visit.

Food and Drinks

Must-Try Dishes

Montenegro, a treasure hidden along the Adriatic coast, provides a gastronomic adventure as rich and diverse as its scenery. From the craggy highlands to the tranquil coastline, the tastes here are a delectable combination of Mediterranean and Balkan influences. Let's get into some must-try foods that will make your taste buds dance with delight.

First, we have Njeguški pršut, a sort of prosciutto from the hamlet of Njeguši. This delicacy is carefully made, with complete pig hind legs salted for three weeks before being air-dried and smoked for many months. The end product is a smokey, delicious delight that goes well with local cheeses and a glass of Montenegrin wine. This may be found in local markets and specialized stores around the nation.

Kačamak, a traditional Montenegrin delicacy, is also a must-try. Made with cornmeal, potatoes, and cheese, it's the epitome of comfort cuisine. Kačamak, usually served in mountain locations and topped with kajmak, a creamy dairy product, is a popular dish.

Buzara is a must-have for seafood lovers. This meal includes shellfish such as mussels or prawns cooked in a rich sauce of white wine, garlic, and parsley. It's a seaside classic, ideal for a warm evening by the water. Many beach eateries offer buzara, so you'll have lots of opportunities to sample it.

Ispod sača is Montenegro's version of a Sunday roast. Meat, often lamb or veal, is slow-cooked with potatoes and vegetables under a metal dome topped with hot coals. As a consequence, the flesh is soft, delicious, and falls right off the bone. This meal is often served at family gatherings and special events.

Don't miss out on black risotto, a visually appealing dish prepared with cuttlefish ink. It's a seaside specialty that's both tasty and visually gorgeous. The risotto is prepared with garlic, white wine, and a hint of nutmeg, giving it a distinct taste that is both rich and delicious. Just be prepared for your teeth to get a little black after indulging!

Finally, there's brav u mlijeku (lamb in milk). This classic recipe consists of slow-cooking lamb in milk with garlic, rosemary, and other herbs. The milk tenderizes the beef, creating a meal that is both soft and savory. It's a bit of a hidden treasure, often found in the northern highlands.

Local Beverages

Montenegro, with its breathtaking surroundings and rich history, has a lovely selection of native drinks that represent its eclectic culture. Whether you're visiting the shore or the mountains, there's a drink for everyone.

The first item on the list is rakija, a powerful fruit brandy that is popular in Montenegrin families. Rakija, produced from a variety of fruits including plums, grapes, and apricots, is often homemade and consumed at social occasions. It's more than simply a drink; it's a gesture of welcome. It's often served in tiny glasses, with a hearty toast.

Montenegro is proud of its wine, and Vranac is no exception. This strong red wine is created from the local Vranac grape, with rich flavors of black cherries and a touch of spice. The finest spot to enjoy Vranac is among the vineyards around Lake Skadar, where you can visit the wineries and try various vintages. The wine goes well with local cuisine, making it a must-try for every tourist.

For a lighter choice, consider Krstač, a crisp white wine native to Montenegro. It's ideal for a warm day, with notes of citrus and green apple. This wine is especially popular in coastal locations, where it pairs nicely with fresh seafood meals.

Nikšićko Pivo is a popular beer among Montenegrins. This beer, brewed in Nikšić, has a pleasant, malty taste and is widely accessible nationwide. A chilled Nikšićko Pivo is an excellent option for resting on the beach or having a meal at a local bar.

For something a little different, try medovina, a traditional honey wine. This sweet, fragrant beverage is created by fermenting honey with water and sometimes adding herbs or spices. It is often consumed at festive events and has a distinct taste that is both rich and calming.

Pelinkovac, a bitter herbal liqueur, is popular in Montenegro. It's made from a mix of herbs, including wormwood, and is noted for its therapeutic benefits and peculiar flavor. It is often offered as a digestif, helping to soothe the stomach after a heavy meal.

Finally, don't miss out on Turkish coffee, which is a strong, unfiltered coffee that many Montenegrins drink every day. This coffee is thick and creamy, and it is often served in tiny cups with a glass of water and a piece of Turkish delight. It's the ideal way to begin the day or unwind at one of Montenegro's lovely cafés.

Top Restaurants and Cafés in the Country

Montenegro, a nation where mountains meet the sea, has a gastronomic landscape as varied as its environment. Whether you're meandering around Kotor's cobblestone alleyways or exploring Durmitor's raw scenery, there are eateries and cafés to suit every taste. Here are a few must-see attractions.

Stari Mlini in Kotor is a must-see. This historic restaurant, housed in a converted flour mill dating back to the 1700s, provides a unique eating experience. It is located in Ljuta bb in Kotor and has a lovely seaside location with a private marina. The restaurant's cuisine includes freshly caught fish and seafood, as well as items from its farm. It's the ideal setting for a romantic supper or a memorable occasion.

Restaurant Vodenica, located in the center of Kolasin, is a welcoming establishment that seems like a home away from home. This restaurant, located in Breze, Kolasin, is well-known for its welcoming atmosphere and rustic appeal.

The menu includes typical Montenegrin foods such as cicvara and polenta, all of which are lovingly made. It is open every day from 9:00 a.m. until 11:00 p.m., giving it an excellent choice for both lunch and supper.

Restoran Koliba is a hidden treasure in the Durmitor area. This restaurant, located at Savin Kuk Bb in Zabljak, serves traditional cuisine and has a warm ambiance. Chef Milica leads the kitchen, which prepares substantial meals ideal for after a day of trekking or skiing. The restaurant is open from June to September and December to March, allowing you to enjoy its offerings in both the summer and winter.

Dvorište is a prominent café and restaurant situated on Jakova Ostojića in Zabljak. It's a terrific location to rest after touring the adjacent national park, thanks to its laid-back atmosphere and tasty meals. The café is open from 11:00 AM to 11:45 PM and serves a variety of foods, from light snacks to big dinners.

If you're in Tivat, check out The Spot, a trendy brasserie-style restaurant on Lustica Bay's waterfront promenade. With unlimited sea views and a cuisine full of savory Asian foods and curries, it's an excellent choice for lunch and supper. The restaurant regularly features live music and DJ evenings, which contribute to its lively environment.

For a taste of luxury, visit Monte Bay Retreat in Perast. This boutique hotel and restaurant has spectacular views of Kotor Bay and serves a cuisine that combines local ingredients with a cosmopolitan flare. It's the perfect place for a leisurely breakfast or a romantic meal, and you can even overnight in one of their tastefully decorated rooms.

Outdoor Adventures and Activities

Hiking and Natural Trails

Montenegro is a hidden jewel in the Balkans with some of Europe's most magnificent hiking and natural paths. This little nation is a haven for adventure lovers, with spectacular scenery ranging from steep mountains to tranquil coastline pathways. Whether you're an experienced hiker or just like a nice stroll in nature, Montenegro offers something for you.

Durmitor National Park's trek to Bobotov Kuk is one of its most well-known hikes. Bobotov Kuk, which stands at 2,523 meters, is Montenegro's highest mountain. The trek is tough but very rewarding, with panoramic views of the surrounding peaks and valleys. The route leads through beautiful woods, past glacier lakes, and up steep hills. It's best undertaken during the summer when the weather is more reliable.

For those who prefer a less demanding activity, the Bay of Kotor has various picturesque routes. The climb to the Sveti Ivan Fortress is a necessity. The walk begins in the historic town of Kotor and goes steeply up the slope, providing breathtaking views of the harbor below. The stronghold itself is an interesting historical monument, with remains going back to the sixth century.

Lovćen National Park, which includes the famed Njegoš Mausoleum, is another excellent alternative. The trail to the mausoleum is very short but steep, with a series of switchbacks rising to the peak. On a clear day, the summit provides a view of the Adriatic Sea. Other routes in the park go through lush woods and past traditional mountain communities.

If you want a multi-day excursion, try the Peaks of the Balkans path. This epic walk crosses three countries—Montenegro, Albania, and Kosovo—and passes through some of the most inaccessible and spectacular terrain in the area. The Montenegrin leg of the path passes through the Prokletije Mountains, often known as the "Accursed Mountains." This is a wild and harsh landscape with towering peaks, deep valleys, and pure rivers.

For a more leisurely experience, the Vrmac Ridge provides a mild trek with breathtaking views of both the Bay of Kotor and Tivat Bay. The track is well-defined and suited for all fitness levels. Along the trip, you'll travel past picturesque towns and old ruins, making it an excellent choice for history aficionados.

No hiking guide in Montenegro would be complete without including Biogradska Gora National Park. This park is home to one of Europe's few surviving primeval woods. The main walk encircles the breathtaking Biogradska Lake, a tranquil area surrounded by tall trees and rich foliage. It's a simple climb, ideal for families or anybody seeking for a relaxing day in nature.

Water Sports

Montenegro's gorgeous Adriatic coastline and steep mountain rivers make it a sanctuary for water sports aficionados. Whether you like the excitement of white-water rafting, the tranquility of sailing, or the adventure of kayaking, this little Balkan nation has a range of adventures to suit all skill levels.

Sailing in Montenegro is a dream come true for many. The Bay of Kotor, widely regarded as one of the world's most beautiful bays, offers an ideal location for sailing. The quiet, pure waters are bordered by high mountains and picturesque medieval villages. You may begin your voyage at the ancient town of Kotor, where marinas are well-equipped and the sailing community is friendly. As you cruise around the bay, you'll see attractive communities such as Perast, with its unique twin islands, and Herceg Novi, which is famed for its energetic atmosphere and gorgeous strongholds. Beyond the bay, the Adriatic Sea provides more demanding sailing conditions, making it perfect for anyone wishing to put their talents to the test.

Kayaking is a great method to explore Montenegro's rivers if you want a more hands-on experience. The Bay of Kotor is once again a popular destination, where you may paddle around the shoreline, finding secret coves and isolated beaches. The placid waters are ideal for novices, while more experienced kayakers may travel farther out to discover the open sea. Lake Skadar, the Balkans' biggest lake, is another excellent kayaking destination. This freshwater lake, shared with Albania, provides a home for biodiversity, notably bird species. Paddling over its peaceful waterways, you'll come across verdant wetlands, old monasteries, and quaint fishing communities.

For adrenaline enthusiasts, rafting on the Tara River is a must-do. The Tara River Canyon, the world's second deepest, provides some of Europe's greatest whitewater rafting opportunities. The river's rapids vary from mild to hard, making it appropriate for both novice and experienced rafters. The drive down the canyon is breathtaking, with crystal-clear waterways, high cliffs, and lush vegetation. The rafting season normally lasts from April to October, with the spring months providing the most exhilarating conditions owing to melting snow in the mountains.

Durmitor National Park offers skiing and winter sports.

Durmitor National Park, located in the heart of Montenegro, turns into a winter paradise the moment the first snowflakes fall. This UNESCO World Heritage site, with its spectacular peaks and beautiful landscapes, provides some of the greatest ski and winter sports experiences in the Balkans.

Žabljak, situated at a height of around 1,500 meters, is the entryway to Durmitor's winter sports. It is the highest town in the Balkans and a popular destination for mountain tourists. The ski season here normally lasts from December to April, with slopes suitable for all skill levels of skiers and snowboarders. The major ski area, Savin Kuk, offers a wide range of courses, from easy slopes for novices to more difficult descents for the expert. The views from the summit are breathtaking, with snow-covered peaks extending as far as the eye can reach.

Žabljak has various ski schools where beginners may learn and improve their technique. There are several equipment rental stores, so you'll be prepared for a day on the slopes. After a day of skiing, the town's quaint cafés and restaurants are the ideal places to warm up and eat substantial Montenegrin cuisine.

Aside from skiing, Durmitor provides a variety of other winter sports. Snowshoeing is a great way to explore the park's calmer areas. Trails weave through old woods and over frozen lakes, providing a tranquil respite from the busy ski slopes. Guided snowshoe walks are provided, offering information about the park's distinctive flora and animals.

Snowmobiling is a popular option for those looking for a more thrilling vacation. Rent snowmobiles in Žabljak and enjoy an exciting trip across the park's challenging landscape. The paths lead you deep into the bush, allowing you to experience Durmitor's raw splendor in winter.

Ice climbing is another thrilling pastime for the daring. Climbers may challenge themselves on the park's ice waterfalls. Local guides provide courses for all ability levels, assuring a safe and exciting experience.

The Durmitor Winter Cup, a series of events including ski races, snowboarding contests, and even ice vehicle racing, is one of the highlights of Durmitor's winter season. In Žabljak, people and tourists enjoy the winter season with a lively atmosphere.

Relaxing at one of Žabljak's wellness facilities is the perfect way to unwind after outdoor activities. Many hotels include spa amenities, such as saunas and hot tubs, where you may relax and relieve sore muscles.

Wildlife watching and eco-tourism

Montenegro's various ecosystems and breathtaking natural beauty make it a wildlife and eco-tourist paradise. This little Balkan nation has a diverse range of environments, including coastal marshes, deep woods, and rocky mountains, each with its flora and wildlife.

Lake Skadar National Park is a popular wildlife-watching destination. This huge freshwater lake, which shares borders with Albania, is a birdwatcher's paradise. There have been over 280 bird species documented here, including the uncommon Dalmatian pelican. The lake's wetlands provide a critical habitat for this and other species, making it one of Europe's most significant bird reserves. Guided boat cruises are an excellent opportunity to see the lake's biodiversity. As you glide along the peaceful waterways, you may see herons, cormorants, and maybe the rare pygmy cormorant.

Biogradska Gora National Park is another hidden treasure for nature enthusiasts. This park, which includes one of Europe's few surviving primeval woods, is a biodiversity hotspot. The old forest, with its towering trees and dense undergrowth, provides a haven for a diverse range of creatures. Deer, wild boar, and foxes are often observed, and if you're fortunate, you could even see a brown bear or a lynx. The park's main attraction, Biogradska Lake, is encircled by a network of hiking paths that provide good opportunities for animal viewing.

For individuals interested in marine life, the Bay of Kotor and the Adriatic Sea provide diverse underwater habitats. The clean, mild seas are home to a variety of fish, sea turtles, and dolphins. Snorkeling and diving tours are popular activities that allow you to see the beautiful marine life up close. The bay's craggy beaches and underwater tunnels are especially spectacular, packed with colorful fish and other marine life.

Montenegro's dedication to eco-tourism is shown by its various protected areas and sustainable tourist projects. Durmitor National Park, a UNESCO World Heritage site, is an excellent example. The park's harsh topography, which includes deep gorges, glacial lakes, and high summits, is ideal for adventure enthusiasts. Eco-friendly hotels and guided excursions promote sustainable practices, preserving the park's natural beauty for future generations.

Another attraction is the Prokletije Mountains, often known as the "Accursed Mountains." This secluded and untamed area is ideal for anyone looking for an off-the-beaten-path experience. Wildlife in the mountains includes chamois, golden eagles, and the uncommon Balkan lynx. Eco-tourism projects in the region aim to preserve the natural environment while offering tourists with a genuine experience of Montenegro's wildness.

Adventure Tours

Montenegro's spectacular vistas and diversified terrain make it an ideal destination for adventurers. From the excitement of ziplining over deep valleys to the tranquil sensation of paragliding over the Adriatic coast, this Balkan jewel has a range of adrenaline-pumping sports to suit all levels of explorers.

Ziplining in Montenegro is an exciting opportunity to see the country's natural beauty from a different viewpoint. The Tara River Canyon, the world's second-deepest canyon, is a famous tourist destination. You may fly above the Tara River's turquoise waters, which are poised high above the canyon bottom. The zipline at the Đurđevića Tara Bridge is famed for its magnificent trip spanning 365 meters. The breathtaking vistas of the canyon and neighboring mountains as you whizz over are memorable.

Paragliding is an excellent choice for people seeking a unique flying activity. Budva, a seaside town, is a popular paragliding destination, with opportunities to take off from the hills and glide over the glittering Adriatic Sea. The views along the coast, with its sandy beaches and old cities, are breathtaking. Experienced instructors guarantee that even inexperienced participants may enjoy this exhilarating sport safely. Lovćen National Park offers excellent paragliding opportunities with panoramic views of the Bay of Kotor and surrounding areas.

If you want to experience more ground-based thrills, Montenegro's rocky terrain is ideal for ATV trips. These journeys take you off the usual route, through deep woods, over rugged terrain, and to spectacular vistas that would otherwise be unreachable. Durmitor National Park is a popular ATV adventure location, with a variety of tough tracks and breathtaking natural scenery. Riding through this UNESCO World Heritage Site, you'll see glacier lakes, deep valleys, and towering peaks.

Canyoning in Montenegro offers a unique water-based adventure experience. The Nevidio Canyon, near Šavnik, is a popular canyoning destination. This tiny, twisting canyon provides an exciting combination of climbing, swimming, and rappelling through crystal-clear rivers and stunning rock formations. Guided excursions are provided, which include all required equipment and guarantee a safe and fun journey.

Rafting down the Tara River is another must-do experience. The river's rapids vary from mild to hard, making it appropriate for both novice and expert rafters. The trek through the Tara River Canyon is spectacular, with its sheer cliffs, rich trees, and clear waterways. The rafting season lasts from April to October, with the spring months providing the most spectacular circumstances owing to melting snow in the mountains.

Beaches and Coastal Experience

Best Beaches to Relax

Montenegro, with its breathtaking Adriatic coastline, is a hidden treasure for beachgoers. Whether you want to relax on a sun-kissed beach or plunge into crystal-clear seas, this Balkan paradise offers something for everyone. Let's take a leisurely walk around some of Montenegro's beautiful beaches.

Jaz Beach is popular with both residents and visitors. This vast beach, only a short drive from Budva, is ideal for individuals who prefer both sand and pebbles. It also hosts the popular Sea Dance Festival, where you may dance the night away with the Adriatic as your background. The beach has many facilities, making it ideal for both families and lone tourists.

For a more private experience, go to Bajova Kula Beach. Nestled in the center of Boka Kotorska Bay, this beach provides a peaceful respite with its clean waters and breathtaking views of the surrounding mountains. It's a little off the beaten route, but that's half of its appeal. The adjacent luxury mansions provide an air of refinement to your beach day.

Przno Beach is another must-see destination. This little, scenic beach near the settlement of Przno is famous for its tranquil seas and easygoing environment. It's an ideal setting for a relaxing day by the shore, with a few small eateries nearby serving fresh seafood and refreshing drinks.

No vacation to Montenegro is complete without a trip to Sveti Stefan Beach. This beautiful beach, with pinkish sands and vistas of the old Sveti Stefan island, is a must-visit. The island is a luxury resort, but the beach is available to the public and has a distinct combination of natural beauty and historical charm.

Ploče Beach in Budva offers a more adventurous experience. Ploče Beach is known for its lively ambiance and crystal-clear seas, making it ideal for swimming, sunbathing, and visiting bustling beach bars. It's a popular site, so it may become busy, but the vibe is contagious, and the vistas are breathtaking.

Hidden coves and secret beaches

Montenegro's coastline is a treasure trove of hidden coves and private beaches, ideal for anyone seeking a piece of paradise away from the masses. Let's go on a tour to find some of these hidden areas where you can actually relax and enjoy the natural beauty.

First on our list is Queen's Beach, located near Miločer. This little, quiet beach is surrounded by lush flora and provides a peaceful retreat from the rush and bustle. The quiet, clear waters are ideal for a relaxing swim, and the beach's serene environment makes it popular with residents.

Next, we visit Drobni Pijesak Beach, which is located between Budva and Petrovac. This pebble beach is less busy and provides a tranquil getaway with crystal-clear seas and breathtaking vistas. The route to this hidden treasure requires a little hiking, but the payoff is a beautiful beach where you can rest in solitude.

For those looking to go a little farther, Perazica Do Beach in Petrovac is a must-see. This hidden treasure, accessible by a beautiful route, has clean seas and rocky surroundings, making it an ideal destination for a day at the beach. The beach is relatively undiscovered, so you're likely to have it all to yourself.

Mirista Beach, located on the Lustica Peninsula, is a quiet area ideal for swimming and snorkeling. The beach is flanked by olive orchards and provides breathtaking views of the Adriatic Sea. Zanjic Beach, located nearby, is a hidden treasure famed for its pristine waters and quiet ambiance.

Both beaches are great for visitors wishing to avoid the more congested areas along the coast.

Fashion Beach in Risan, located in the northern portion of Kotor Bay, provides a calmer alternative to Budva and Kotor's crowded beaches. This pebbled beach is popular with locals and provides all you need for a relaxing day by the sea. The beach is separated into three portions: the center area is owned by a hotel, while the left and right sections are available to the public.

Finally, for a genuinely off-the-beaten-path experience, visit Buljarica Beach, south of Petrovac. This beach is less developed and provides a more rustic experience, making it ideal for individuals who like nature and prefer less crowds. The lengthy stretch of sand and stones is great for a quiet day at the beach, with lots of room to spread out and relax.

Snorkeling and scuba diving spots

Montenegro's Adriatic coast is a diver's dream, thanks to its clean waters and abundant marine life. Whether you're an experienced diver or a first-time snorkeler, there's something for everyone. Let's have a look at some of the top underwater exploration places in this beautiful Balkan nation.

Blue Cave, located on the Lustica Peninsula, is a must-see. This natural beauty is accessible by boat and provides an ethereal experience with its sparkling blue seas. The cave's unusual lighting effects make it popular among snorkelers and divers alike. Early mornings are the greatest time to come since the sunlight casts fascinating colors of blue within the cave.

For anyone interested in exploring shipwrecks, Kotor Bay is the place to be. The port is home to various wrecks, including the legendary Tihany, a Hungarian cargo ship that sunk during World War II. The wreck is located at a depth of around 40 meters, making it ideal for experienced divers. The bay's tranquil waters and rich history make it an intriguing destination for underwater research.

Mamula Island, at the entrance to Kotor Bay, provides another wonderful diving experience. The island is surrounded by crystal-pure seas filled with marine life. Divers may explore the underwater caverns and tunnels, which are home to a wide range of fish and other marine critters. The island itself has a fascinating history, which adds another element of fascination to your dive.

Plavi Horizonti Beach offers a more peaceful snorkeling experience. This beach, on the Lustica Peninsula, is notable for its beautiful, shallow waters and sandy bottom. It's an excellent choice for families and novices, with an abundance of marine life visible only a short swim from the beach. The beach is also outfitted with facilities, making it an ideal location for a day of snorkeling.

Petrovac is another excellent location for snorkeling and diving. The town's beaches are flanked by rocky outcrops and underwater tunnels, which provide several options for exploration. The waters here are clean and tranquil, making it ideal for seeing colorful fish and other marine life. Don't miss the opportunity to dive at the adjacent Katic and Sveta Nedjelja islands, which have bright underwater landscapes and a diverse range of aquatic species.

For those looking for a more daring dive, Bigovo Bay is a rough and less crowded option. The bay's rugged shoreline and underwater caverns are ideal for exploration, and the clear waters provide good visibility. It's a little off the usual road, but the spectacular diving conditions are well worth the journey.

Coastal Towns To Explore

Montenegro's coastline is a patchwork of little settlements, each with its own distinct personality and appeal. Let's take a leisurely tour of some of the most fascinating seaside communities you won't want to miss.

Kotor is a hidden treasure located in the middle of the Bay of Kotor. This historical village, with its meandering lanes and antique buildings, seems like a step back in time. The magnificent San Giovanni Fortress provides stunning views of the harbor and the terracotta roofs below. Kotor's ancient town is a UNESCO World Heritage site, and it's clear why. The combination of Venetian architecture and breathtaking natural landscape makes it a must-see.

Perast, a peaceful town brimming with Mediterranean beauty, is just a short drive away. The town's seafront is surrounded by stone palaces from bygone eras, many of which have been transformed into luxury hotels and restaurants. Perast is also the entryway to the historic islands of Our Lady of the Rocks and Saint George, which are ideal for a quick boat ride.

Budva is the most lively of Montenegro's beach cities. Budva is a popular tourist destination because of its bustling nightlife and stunning beaches. The old town, with its tiny alleys and historic walls, contrasts sharply with the contemporary beach resorts that border the shore. Budva's beaches, such as Mogren and Jaz, are among the finest in the nation, including a mix of sand and pebbles and crystal-clear seas.

Herceg Novi, located at the entrance to the Bay of Kotor, offers a more relaxed atmosphere. This town is sometimes ignored by visitors, yet it's a hidden treasure with its beautiful countryside, medieval strongholds, and attractive old town. The seven-kilometer-long beachfront promenade is ideal for a relaxing walk, while the adjoining Igalo beach is ideal for sunbathing and swimming.

Tivat is another seaside town worth seeing. While Tivat lacks the old-world elegance of Kotor and Budva, it more than compensates with its contemporary port, Porto Montenegro. This opulent complex is home to upmarket stores, restaurants, and hotels, making it an excellent starting point for exploring the surrounding region. The town itself is tiny and simple to traverse, with lots of open areas and a laid-back attitude.

Ulcinj, located farther south, has a very different feel. Ulcinj is a popular destination for younger visitors due to its vast sandy beaches and active nightlife. The ancient town, built on a hill overlooking the sea, is a tangle of small alleys and medieval structures. Ulcinj's beaches, including Velika Plaza, are among the longest in Montenegro, providing enough room to rest and unwind.

Montenegro Beach Resorts and Luxury Stays

Montenegro's coastline is lined with opulent resorts and exquisite accommodations that appeal to every want and fancy. Montenegro offers everything, whether you want a peaceful getaway or a bustling coastal break. Let's have a look at some of the best beach resorts and luxury accommodations in this beautiful nation.

Only Portonovi represents the pinnacle of luxury. Nestled at the entrance of Boka Bay, this resort provides breathtaking views of the Adriatic Sea and the surrounding mountains. The resort offers luxurious accommodations, private villas, and a world-class spa. The dining selections are exceptional, with an emphasis on fresh, locally sourced cuisine. The private beach and marina give an added level of privacy.

Aman Sveti Stefan is a must-see for individuals who value history as well as luxury. This renowned resort is located on a gorgeous island connected to the mainland by a small isthmus. The resort's stone cottages and rooms have been carefully refurbished, providing a unique combination of historic beauty and contemporary luxury. The exclusive beaches and crystal-clear seas make it an ideal destination for leisure.

Regent Porto Montenegro in Tivat is another popular option among luxury tourists. This hotel, located in the middle of Porto Montenegro's harbor, provides breathtaking views of the sea and neighboring mountains. The rooms and suites are tastefully decorated, with an emphasis on comfort and flair. The hotel also has a magnificent spa, many great dining choices, and a stunning pool area.

If you want a more private experience, Villa Geba in Sveti Stefan is a boutique hotel that provides that. With just a few rooms, our hotel offers a customized and unique experience. The rooms are attractively designed, and the hotel's infinity pool provides stunning views of the Adriatic Sea. The on-site restaurant offers gourmet food, making it ideal for a romantic trip.

The Dukley Hotel & Resort in Budva is a great alternative for families. This resort has big apartments and villas ideal for families and parties. The resort's own beach, various pools, and children's club guarantee that everyone has a good time. The on-site restaurants provide a wide range of eating choices, from casual to upscale dining.

The Chedi Lustica Bay is another notable resort. This resort, located in the recently created Lustica Bay region, combines contemporary comfort with a gorgeous environment. The rooms and suites are spacious and attractively built, with big balconies providing panoramic views of the sea. The resort has a private beach, a variety of eating choices, and a luxury spa.

Mamula Island Hotel provides an experience unlike any other. This hotel is situated on a tiny island in the Bay of Kotor, in a historic Austro-Hungarian fort. The hotel has been wonderfully refurbished, blending traditional beauty with contemporary elegance. The island's isolated beaches and pristine seas make it ideal for a relaxing getaway.

Practical tips for tourists

Money is important

When it comes to managing your funds in Montenegro, there are a few crucial points to remember to guarantee a smooth and stress-free stay.

Montenegro's currency is the euro (€). This makes things easier if you're coming from another euro-using nation, but otherwise, you'll need to convert your money. Euro notes exist in denominations of 5, 10, 20, 50, 100, 200, and 500, however the bigger denominations are seldom used. Coin denominations vary from 1 and 2 euros to 1, 2, 5, 10, 20, and 50 cents.

ATMs are generally accessible in cities and towns, so you should have no problem locating one unless you go to extremely distant places. However, be mindful that ATMs often issue big denomination notes, which might be inconvenient for minor transactions. It's a good idea to split these bigger bills at your hotel or a larger retailer.

When withdrawing cash, always ask to be charged in euros rather than your own currency. This avoids the typically disadvantageous exchange rates provided by ATMs. Also, avoid foreign exchange counters at airports and hotels, which tend to charge greater fees and provide less favorable rates.

Most hotels, restaurants, and stores take credit and debit cards, however, smaller places and markets may need cash. To avoid additional expenses, choose a card that does not have international transaction fees.

Tipping is not as customary in Montenegro as it is in other nations, although it is growing more popular, particularly in tourist regions. In restaurants and cafés, rounding up the amount or giving a 10% tip is welcomed. Taxi drivers often round up to the closest euro. Hotel employees, such as porters and housekeepers, would appreciate a modest tip for excellent service.

Internet and Connectivity

Staying connected in Montenegro is simple, whether you're exploring the cobbled alleyways of Kotor or trekking in the steep mountains of Durmitor. Here's how to get your internet fix while visiting this Balkan treasure.

First, let's discuss about SIM cards. Montenegro's three primary mobile providers are One (previously Telenor), T-Mobile, and M: tel. Each provides a variety of prepaid SIM cards designed for vacationers, making it simple to remain connected without breaking the budget. You can get a SIM card at the airport, in large cities, and even at certain petrol stations and kiosks. Prices are cheap, with packages beginning at €10 for a week of data, which is sufficient for the majority of tourists.

If you want to use a lot of data—perhaps to publish those magnificent Adriatic sunset photos—consider One's tourist packages. They provide generous data allocations, ideal for social media lovers. For example, 500GB for a week costs €10, while 1TB for a month costs €20. These packages also contain call and text allowances, ensuring that you are covered for local communication.

Wi-Fi is commonly accessible across Montenegro, particularly in metropolitan areas. Most hotels, cafés, and restaurants have free Wi-Fi, however the quality varies. In more distant regions, the connection may be intermittent, so a solid mobile data package is a smart backup. If you work remotely or need a consistent connection, consider staying in hotels that particularly promise high-speed internet.

For individuals who like to remain connected without changing SIM cards, eSIMs are a practical solution. You may buy and activate an eSIM online before you travel, guaranteeing you're connected as soon as you land. This is especially useful while traveling between countries since it eliminates the need to purchase a new SIM card at each stop.

Safety and Health Precautions

When it comes to safety and health in Montenegro, there are a few things you should keep in mind to make your stay both pleasurable and stress-free.

Montenegro is a relatively secure place, with low crime rates and pleasant residents. Petty crimes, such as pickpocketing, may occur in busy tourist locations, so keep careful. Keep your possessions safe, particularly in popular areas such as marketplaces and public transportation. To keep your valuables handy, always wear a money belt or carry a safe bag.

Montenegro's healthcare system is good, especially in metropolitan regions. Public hospitals and clinics are available, however for more critical problems, private healthcare facilities are advised. It's a good idea to obtain travel insurance that covers medical expenditures since this will allow you to access private treatment if necessary.

Pharmacies are well-stocked, and you can get most common prescriptions without a prescription.

If you want to engage in outdoor activities such as hiking or water sports, take the required measures. The terrain may be rough, and weather conditions can change quickly in the highlands. Always advise someone about your intentions and planned return time. For aquatic sports, be sure you choose trustworthy operators that observe safety standards.

Montenegro's tap water is typically safe to drink, however bottled water is commonly available for those with sensitive stomachs. Food hygiene standards are high, and you may eat local food without anxiety. To reduce the risk of foodborne disease, dine at crowded, well-reviewed restaurants.

There are no special immunization requirements in Montenegro, however, regular vaccinations should be kept up to date. If you are traveling from a country with yellow fever, you may be required to produce evidence of immunization.

Finally, Montenegro's environment can be rather hot in the summer, so keeping hydrated and using sunscreen is crucial. Insect repellent is also recommended, particularly if you're visiting rural regions or spending time outside in the evening.

How To Avoid Tourist Traps

Navigating Montenegro without falling into typical tourist traps might make your vacation more genuine and pleasant. Here are some pointers to help you discover the genuine Montenegro.

First, avoid heavily commercialized regions. While sites like Kotor and Budva are certainly attractive, they may get overcrowded with visitors, particularly during the summer. Instead, visit lesser-known jewels such as Perast, a quaint town with breathtaking views of the Bay of Kotor, or Herceg Novi, which has a more relaxed attitude and great coastline walks.

When eating, avoid places with bilingual menus and pushy promoters. These establishments often cater to visitors and might be pricey. Instead, seek places where the locals eat. Konobas (traditional Montenegrin pubs) are excellent choices for real food. Enjoy foods like Njeguški pršut (smoked ham) and kačamak (a substantial potato and cheese dish). Ask locals for ideas; they're typically eager to share their favorite sites.

Shopping for souvenirs may be a minefield. Instead of shopping at generic trinket shops, go to local markets or artisan businesses. Cetinje, for example, offers one-of-a-kind handcrafted products, local wines, and rakija (a powerful fruit liquor). These provide more meaningful souvenirs and benefit local artists.

Avoid extensively marketed trips and excursions. Instead, hire a vehicle and explore at your own time. Montenegro's modest size makes it ideal for road excursions. Drive through the breathtaking scenery of Durmitor National Park or follow the picturesque road along the Adriatic coast. If you like trekking, the paths surrounding Lake Skadar and the Prokletije Mountains provide stunning views without people.

Accommodation may be another place where travelers get imprisoned. Large hotels in popular tourist destinations may be pricey and lack individuality. Choose guesthouses or family-run B&Bs, which provide a more personalized experience and often include cooked breakfast. Staying in tiny towns or villages might provide a more real experience.

Finally, be aware of busy tourist seasons. Visiting during the shoulder seasons (spring and fall) allows you to escape crowds and enjoy a more calm environment. The weather is still great, and you'll have a higher chance of meeting residents rather than other visitors.

Useful Apps for Montenegrin Travel

Navigating Montenegro using the proper applications may make your vacation easier and more fun. Here's a list of key necessary applications to download before you go on your vacation.

First and foremost, Maps. It is very useful for offline navigation. Montenegro's twisting roads and secret paths are best explored with a good map, and this app allows you to download comprehensive maps for offline usage. Perfect for those times when you're deep in the mountains or touring distant communities with no reception.

Booking.com and Airbnb are the go-to applications for booking accommodations. They provide a broad choice of accommodations, from small guesthouses in Kotor to magnificent villas on the Adriatic coast. Both applications let you restrict searches based on your preferences, ensuring that you locate the ideal location to stay.

Moovit is tremendously beneficial for navigating Montenegro's public transportation system. It gives real-time information on bus timetables and routes, allowing you to easily navigate places like as Podgorica and Budva. Rentalcars.com is a useful tool for comparing pricing and booking your rental car.

To remain connected, One (previously Telenor) provides user-friendly software for managing mobile data and filling up your prepaid SIM card. This is especially beneficial if you're using one of their tourist packages, which provide huge data allowances at a fair fee.

If you want to explore Montenegro's natural beauty, Komoot is an excellent app for hikers and bikers. It includes comprehensive trail maps and user-generated suggestions to help you organize your outdoor trips. Whether you're climbing the heights of Durmitor or riding around Lake Skadar, Komoot has you covered.

TripAdvisor and Yelp are wonderful resources for local restaurants and activities. They provide evaluations and suggestions for restaurants, cafés, and sights, allowing you to avoid tourist traps and find hidden treasures. You may also book excursions and activities straight from these apps, making it simple to arrange your trip.

Finally, the Montenegro Village Explorer app is a unique tool for exploring rural Montenegro. It takes you through over 230 rural families, providing real experiences and insights into traditional Montenegrin life.

Laws and Regulations For Visitors

Local Laws Every Tourist Should Know

Montenegro, with its magnificent Adriatic coastline and rocky mountains, is a treasure waiting to be found. But, before you delve into its medieval towns and stunning beaches, it's important to understand certain local rules and traditions to guarantee a smooth and pleasurable journey.

Driving and Road Etiquette

Driving in Montenegro can be an experience in itself, with winding mountain roads that provide beautiful vistas. However, it is important to know that Montenegrins drive on the right side of the road. The minimum driving age is 18, and seatbelts are required for all passengers. Using a cell phone while driving is completely illegal unless you have a hands-free device. Speed restrictions are strictly enforced, and traffic cameras are widely distributed, so it's better to follow the regulations to avoid penalties.

Alcohol and Smoking Regulations

Montenegro's stance toward alcohol is generally lenient, yet there are still restrictions to obey. The legal drinking age is eighteen. Drinking in public areas is typically discouraged, and driving under the influence is a criminal violation. The blood alcohol limit for drivers is 0.03%, and the consequences for exceeding it are harsh.

Smoking is prevalent in Montenegro, however, it is prohibited in enclosed public venues, such as restaurants and bars. However, many businesses offer designated smoking areas, so always ask before lighting up.

Respect for nature and wildlife.

Montenegro's natural beauty is one of its main attractions, and the residents take environmental conservation seriously. When visiting national parks or protected areas, stay on approved pathways, avoid trash, and do not disturb the animals. Fines for harming or polluting natural areas may be high, so tread cautiously and protect the environment.

Social Etiquettes and Customs

Montenegrins are recognized for their friendliness and hospitality. When meeting someone, a strong handshake and direct eye contact are expected. In more formal circumstances, a small bow could be suitable. It is customary to wait for your host to start eating before beginning your dinner and to thank them for their hospitality.

Emergency Contacts:

In case of an emergency, contact 112 for general help. For particular services, call the police at 122, the fire department at 123, or medical emergency at 124. These services are efficient and dependable, ensuring that aid is always available when required.

Rules for Photography and Drones

Montenegro, with its breathtaking vistas and ancient charm, is a photographer's paradise. But before you start clicking pictures or flying your drone aloft, you need to be informed of the local norms and restrictions to guarantee you capture the beauty of this Balkan jewel without incident.

Photography Etiquette:

Montenegro is a nation that cherishes privacy and tradition. When shooting people, always get permission first, particularly in rural places where traditions are firmly ingrained. Locals are typically nice and may even pose for photos, although it is polite to ask. Photography may be banned or fee-based at religious places such as the Ostrog Monastery or the various Orthodox churches. Always seek signage or ask a staff member to prevent confusion.

Drone Regulations

Drones are legal to fly in Montenegro, although there are certain restrictions. The Montenegrin Civil Aviation Authority (CAA) monitors drone activities and has established specific procedures to protect safety and privacy. First and foremost, all drones must be registered with the CAA, and operators must acquire approval before each flight. This applies to both enthusiasts and business users.

Drones may only be flown during daylight hours and must stay in the operator's line of sight. Drone flights have a maximum height of 150 meters (492 feet) and must maintain a minimum distance of 30 meters (98 feet) from people, animals, and structures. Flying over busy locations, such as cities or popular beaches, is normally illegal unless granted specific authorization. This is to safeguard the safety and privacy of all residents and guests.

Importing Drones

If you want to bring a drone into Montenegro, you must get an import authorization from the Ministry of Economy. This procedure guarantees that all drones entering the nation comply with safety regulations and are properly registered. Failure to do so may result in penalties or the seizure of your equipment.

Respecting Privacy

Privacy is a major problem in Montenegro, and drone operators must be aware of this. Avoid flying over private property or taking photos of individuals without their permission. The use of drones for shooting or photographing in sensitive places, such as government buildings or military installations, is highly forbidden and may result in serious fines.

Practical Tips

Check the weather before heading out with your camera or drone. Montenegro's coastline locations may be windy, which may impair your drone's stability. Also, be mindful of local wildlife and avoid harming it, particularly in national parks like as Durmitor or Biogradska Gora.

Montenegro's Smoking and Alcohol Laws

Montenegro, with its gorgeous surroundings and lively culture, combines history and contemporary effortlessly. However, when it comes to smoking and drinking, there are some regulations and norms that every visitor should be aware of in order to have a smooth and happy vacation.

Smoking Regulations

Montenegro has taken major measures to reduce smoking in public places. As of August 2019, smoking is prohibited in all enclosed public spaces, including restaurants, cafés, and bars. The lone exception to this law is casinos, which still allow smoking. This regulation is intended to protect nonsmokers from secondhand smoke and create a healthier atmosphere. If you smoke, seek approved smoking locations, which are typically clearly signposted. Violations of these restrictions may result in significant penalties, so it is advisable to light up only where it is permitted.

Alcohol Laws

Montenegro's alcohol policy is rather permissive, yet there are still laws to obey. The legal drinking age is 18 and is tightly enforced. When buying alcohol or entering pubs and nightclubs, you may be requested to produce your identity. Public drunkenness is frowned upon, and although drinking is part of the local culture, it is essential to do it safely.

Local Drinking Culture

Alcohol plays an important part in Montenegrin social life. Croatia is well-known for its wine, with prominent varietals including Vranac (a powerful red) and Krstač (a crisp white). Another popular drink is rakija, a powerful fruit brandy that is often prepared at home and served at festivals. When given a drink, it is courteous to accept it as a sign of hospitality. If you choose not to drink, a simple, courteous denial is typically acceptable.

Practical Tips

When visiting Montenegro, it is best to be aware of these restrictions to prevent unpleasant surprises. Always carry identification, particularly if you seem young, and follow smoking regulations to guarantee a good experience for everybody. Enjoy the local drinks, but remember to drink responsibly and follow the rules and traditions of this wonderful nation.

Public Behavior

Montenegro, with its combination of Adriatic elegance and Balkan roughness, is a land where traditions are strong. To make the most of your vacation, it's vital to learn local norms and mannerisms, which will help you get along with the people.

Greetings and Social Etiquette

Montenegrins are recognized for their friendliness and hospitality. When greeting someone, a strong handshake and direct eye contact are standard. In more formal situations, such as greeting an elder or someone of greater rank, a small bow may be acceptable. It is also usual to address persons by their titles, such as Mr. or Mrs., followed by their last name.

Dinner Etiquette

When welcomed into a Montenegrin house, it is customary to provide a little gift, such as flowers or a bottle of wine. Wait for your host to begin eating before you start, and always show your appreciation for their hospitality. Montenegrins are proud of their cuisine, thus compliments are always welcomed.

Dress Code:

While Montenegro is very liberal, humility is valued, particularly in religious and rural communities. When entering churches or mosques, both men and women should cover their shoulders and avoid wearing shorts or skirts that go above the knee. Dressing modestly is also recommended while visiting traditional communities or participating in outdoor activities.

Public Behavior

Public shows of love are typically frowned upon, particularly in more conservative communities. To prevent drawing unwanted attention, such displays should be kept to a minimum. Additionally, being loud or boisterous in public places is considered impolite. Montenegrins cherish peace and quiet, so keep your voice down in public settings.

Respect for elders.

Respecting elders is an important aspect of Montenegrin culture. Always give your seat to an elderly person on public transportation, and be cordial in your dealings. Elders are highly revered, and treating them with reverence will gain you respect in return.

Environmental Respect

Montenegro's natural beauty is one of its main attractions, and the residents take environmental conservation seriously. When visiting national parks or protected areas, stay on approved pathways, avoid trash, and do not disturb the animals. Fines for harming or polluting natural areas may be high, so tread cautiously and protect the environment.

Punctuality

Punctuality is very important in Montenegro. Whether you're meeting someone for coffee or attending a business meeting, it's important to appear on time. Being late is considered rude and may have a negative impact.

Sustainable and Responsible Travel

Supporting Local Businesses.

Supporting local businesses in Montenegro is more than simply buying; it's about getting to know the heart and spirit of this beautiful Balkan nation. From the busy marketplaces of Podgorica to the quiet artisan stores of Kotor, every purchase tells a story and helps to realize a dream.

Montenegro's small and medium-sized companies (SMEs) are the backbone of the economy. These companies, which are generally owned by families, provide a unique view into the country's culture and customs. Whether it's a handmade piece of jewelry, a bottle of locally produced wine, or a meal at a family-run restaurant, supporting these companies helps to preserve Montenegrin tradition.

The European Bank for Reconstruction and Development (EBRD) and the European Union (EU) have been helpful in assisting these businesses. They give the capital needed for local companies to develop by combining loans and grants. This assistance enables firms to replace their equipment, enhance energy efficiency, and comply with EU requirements, making them more competitive both locally and globally.

In the seaside town of Bar, the local government has made substantial initiatives to help businesses. The municipality has dedicated significant monies to assist the launch or growth of private firms via programs such as the Business Development Support Program. This initiative not only provided employment but also developed a feeling of community and trust between local officials and businesspeople.

Walking through the streets of Montenegro, you will see that each town has its own distinct offerings. In Cetinje, the old royal capital, you may tour workshops where traditional crafts are preserved. Žabljak, located in the north, provides locally created items inspired by the Durmitor National Park's rough landscape.

How to reduce your environmental impact.

Reducing your environmental effect while visiting Montenegro is not just a conscientious decision, but also a chance to genuinely connect with the country's natural beauty and culture. Here's how you can make an impact:

Begin with your accommodation. Choose eco-friendly hotels or guesthouses that value sustainability. Many localities in Montenegro are already adopting green techniques, such as solar panels and water-saving measures. Staying in these areas not only helps to minimize your carbon footprint but also supports companies that care about the environment.

When it comes to getting about, consider using public transportation, cycling, or walking. Montenegro's tiny size makes it ideal for exploring on foot or by bicycle. Not only will you minimize emissions, but you will also get the opportunity to see the country's breathtaking scenery up close. If you need to hire a vehicle, consider hybrid or electric possibilities.

Eating locally is another effective strategy to reduce your environmental footprint. Montenegro's marketplaces are filled with fresh, locally grown products. By eating locally, you reduce the carbon emissions connected with transportation. You'll also get to enjoy the genuine tastes of Montenegrin cuisine.

Montenegro is endowed with magnificent natural parks and reserves. When visiting these locations, stay on established routes to prevent disrupting animal and plant life. Carry reusable water bottles and bags to help decrease plastic waste. Many parks have programs in place to educate visitors about environmental protection, so make use of these tools.

Supporting local companies that value sustainability is also essential. Look for stores and craftspeople that utilize environmentally friendly products and techniques. This benefits not just the environment, but also the local economy.

Finally, be cautious of your energy use. Simple acts such as turning off lights and unplugging gadgets while not in use may have a significant impact. Many lodgings now provide advice on how to be more energy-efficient during your stay.

Community-based tourism

Community-based tourism in Montenegro provides a unique opportunity to immerse oneself in the country's rich culture and breathtaking scenery. This kind of travel enables you to interact with local people, learn about their customs, and contribute directly to their livelihoods.

Stay in the lovely town of Njeguši, hidden in the highlands above Kotor, with local families that welcome guests. You'll get a flavor of traditional Montenegrin life here, from savoring handmade prosciutto and cheese to learning about the process of distilling rakija (local brandy). The villagers' warmth is real, and you will leave with a better knowledge of their way of life.

Heading north, the town of Plav provides another unique experience. Plav, surrounded by the gorgeous Prokletije mountains, serves as the entryway to some of Montenegro's most beautiful natural surroundings. Local guides may lead you on walks into the mountains, where you'll find secret lakes and old woods. Staying in a guesthouse here means enjoying delicious, home-cooked meals and hearing tales about the region's history and mythology.

In the seaside town of Ulcinj, community-based tourism takes on a new character. This region is noted for its unique cultural legacy, which includes influences from Ottoman, Venetian, and Slavic cultures. You may accompany local fishermen on their boats, learn traditional fishing skills, and even try your hand at catching your own meal. The town's colorful markets are also a must-see, where you can purchase fresh vegetables and handcrafted items straight from the craftspeople.

Montenegro's dedication to community-based tourism is shown in its support for these programs. The National Tourism Organization of Montenegro and other non-governmental organizations (NGOs) collaborate with local communities to establish sustainable tourism practices.

This guarantees that tourism helps the locals rather than simply major enterprises.

Ethical souvenir shopping

Ethical souvenir buying in Montenegro is a wonderful opportunity to take home a piece of this lovely nation while also helping local artists and protecting cultural heritage. Here's how to purchase safely for genuinely unique souvenirs.

Begin your adventure in the picturesque ancient town of Kotor. There are a number of stores here that sell handcrafted products. Look for traditional Montenegrin headgear, known as "kapa," which is historically significant and symbolic. These hats are often produced by local artisans who follow traditional techniques handed down through generations. By purchasing one, you are not only acquiring a hat but also helping the preservation of a cultural tradition.

Budva's old town is a treasure trove of environmentally friendly stores. These shops prioritize sustainability, selling things manufactured from natural and recyclable materials. You may buy stunning handcrafted jewelry, organic cotton apparel, and even eco-friendly cosmetics. These goods are ideal presents and reflect Montenegro's increasing dedication to environmental sustainability.

For a flavor of Montenegro, visit the markets in Podgorica or Bar. You may get locally made honey, olive oil, and rakija, a traditional fruit brandy. These items are often produced by tiny family enterprises utilizing traditional techniques. They are not only tasty, but they also benefit local agriculture by preserving traditional agricultural techniques.

Njeguši village offers a one-of-a-kind experience. This little community is famed for its Njeguški pršut, a sort of smoked ham and a local delicacy. The ham is cured with sea salt and pure mountain air, giving it a unique taste. Buying directly from the producers assures that you get an original product while also helping local farmers.

Ulcinj, a seaside town, is home to magnificent handcrafted textiles and pottery. These objects are often made by local artists who employ traditions passed down through generations. Buying these items helps preserve traditional crafts alive and provides a living for the craftspeople.

When shopping for souvenirs, always search for things marked as fair trade or sustainably made. This assures that the items are manufactured responsibly and that the craftsmen are appropriately compensated for their efforts. Avoid mass-produced commodities, which are often imported and do not benefit the local economy.

Wildlife Protection and Conservation Initiatives

Montenegro, with its spectacular terrain and abundant biodiversity, has emerged as a hub for wildlife protection and conservation activities. The country's dedication to maintaining its natural heritage is shown by a variety of projects aimed at protecting its distinctive flora and wildlife.

One of the most important initiatives is the creation of Marine Protected Areas (MPAs) along the Adriatic coast. These regions, including Platamuni, Katič, and Stari Ulcinj, are vital for protecting marine biodiversity. These MPAs, funded by the Global Environment Facility and the United Nations Environment Programme, help to safeguard ecosystems from overfishing, pollution, and other threats. The effort not only protects marine species but also maintains the health of coastal ecosystems, which are critical to local residents.

Inland, Montenegro has made progress in conserving its rivers. In response to local and international activism, the government has suspended the building of many minor hydropower facilities. This ruling safeguards rivers including the Bukovica, Bistrica, and Murinska, which are critical for biodiversity conservation and ecological services. These rivers sustain a diverse range of animals and are vital to the lives of many Montenegrins.

Durmitor National Park, a UNESCO World Heritage site, is another key component of Montenegro's conservation efforts. This park provides a haven for a variety of wildlife, including the endangered Balkan Lynx. Conservation activities in this area are focused on habitat protection, anti-poaching measures, and community participation. The park's administration collaborates closely with local people to promote sustainable tourism and animal conservation.

The Montenegrin Dolphin Research Project is a volunteer-led initiative that undertakes regular surveys to monitor dolphin numbers and promote maritime conservation. By employing volunteers, the initiative promotes awareness and creates a feeling of responsibility among both residents and tourists.

Efforts to prevent illicit logging and promote sustainable forestry practices continue. These measures are critical to protecting habitats for animals such as the brown bear and gray wolf. The Montenegrin Center for Bird Protection and Research (CZIP) is critical to the conservation of bird species and their habitats. They monitor biodiversity, educate citizens, and collaborate with other environmental conservation groups.

Scan the QRCODE to view full Montenegro map

Made in United States
Troutdale, OR
01/30/2025

28492409R10090